Estate Planning in Texas

Fourth Edition

Leslie Dillon Thomas

THOMAS-WALTERS, PLLC

ABOUT THE AUTHOR

Leslie Dillon Thomas is a founding member, managing partner, and an estate planning attorney with THOMAS-WALTERS, PLLC. She received her business degree from Texas A&M University in 1990, and graduated *magna cum laude* from South Texas College of Law in 1993, where she was the Assistant Editor of the *Law Review* and, upon graduation, received the faculty award for her exemplary character, perseverance, and legal ability. She has received numerous awards and recognitions throughout her career, including being repeatedly named one of the top estate planning attorneys in Fort Worth, one of the top ten estate planning attorneys in Texas, and recognized by *Who's Who in America*. She is often asked to speak at conferences and seminars pertaining to important estate planning issues. Leslie is licensed to practice law in multiple states and focuses her practice exclusively in the area of estate planning.

Published by: THOMAS-WALTERS, PLLC
1701 River Run, Suite 1010
Fort Worth, TX 76107

Fourth edition.

ACKNOWLEDGMENTS

We have not attempted to cite in the text all of the authorities and sources consulted in the preparation of this book. To do so would require more space than is available. The list would include departments of the county, state and federal governments, libraries, internet sources, and many individual clients.

DISCLAIMER

This book is designed to offer general information about the subjects covered. If you need legal, financial, tax, accounting, or other professional assistance, you should seek the services of a competent professional.

Every effort has been made to make this book as complete and accurate as possible. However, there could be mistakes, both typographical and in content. Therefore, this text should be used only as a general guide and not as the final source of estate planning law in Texas. Further, the information on estate planning in this book is only up to date as of the printing of this book.

The purpose of this book is to educate and entertain. The author shall have neither liability nor responsibility to any person or entity with respect to any loss or damage caused or allegedly caused, directly or indirectly, by the information contained in this book.

Dedication

I dedicate this book to my husband, Chad, who is forever supportive of all my endeavors and is always there to pick me up whenever I may fall; to my children, Meredith and James, to whom I have dedicated all of my efforts in life and who continue to inspire me daily; and to my parents, Audrey and John Dillon, without whom none of my successes in life would be possible.

Table of Contents

Chapter 1

What Is Estate Planning?

ELIMINATING UNCERTAINTY ABOUT THE FUTURE

You may have heard the phrase, "getting your affairs in order." That is a simple, but accurate, definition of estate planning. No one knows how long they are going to live, whether they will become incapacitated during their lifetime and need long-term medical care, or when they will die. You must plan now for these uncertainties, or the end results could be financially and emotionally devastating for you and your loved ones.

Believe it or not, nearly everyone has an estate. Your estate consists of everything you own at the time of your death, such as your car, home, checking and savings accounts, stocks and other securities, life insurance policies, and other real estate interests.

Many people do not like to think about death or what will become of their families, loved ones, or assets when they pass away. For many it can seem daunting, confusing, and depressing. However, establishing a customized and comprehensive estate plan is a very attainable goal for everyone. An estate plan not only provides instructions stating who you want to receive your assets when you die, but also provides details about what they are to receive and when they are to receive their inheritance. A comprehensive estate plan will include these stipulations and will be structured to avoid unnecessary taxes, legal fees, and court expenses.

Is Estate Planning for Everyone?

Many people procrastinate when it comes to estate planning because they think they do not own enough assets, are not old enough, or have plenty of time to take care of such matters. A common myth associated with estate planning is that it is just for retired individuals or the very wealthy, but this could not be further from the truth. No one can predict how long they will live. Illnesses and accidents can happen to anyone and at any time. Some wealthy individuals are more likely to think about ways to preserve their assets, but others with a more modest estate should also make estate planning a priority, since a loss to them is more impactful. Procrastinating could cause tremendous turmoil and confusion when you die, and your loved ones will be left to pick up the pieces.

In early 2016, the musician Prince died with an estate valued in the millions of dollars, but left no plan in place to establish beneficiaries or to direct the disposition of his assets. Many other famous people have also died without an estate plan in place, including Abraham Lincoln and Texas billionaire Howard Hughes. In fact, the majority of Americans have not taken any steps to plan for their estates. A 2015 Harris Poll found that sixty-four percent of Americans have not put a plan in place for their estate, and other surveys indicate that up to seventy-five percent of Americans die without even establishing a will. Many people say they are too busy, that estate planning is too complicated, or they did not think they had enough money or assets to justify an estate plan. The truth is, if you have a home or any other assets and you want to make sure that those assets go to whom you want and when you want when you pass away, then you need an estate plan.

READER ALERT: Most Americans pass away without any estate plan in place, leaving their loved ones to pick up the pieces and sort out the distribution of their assets.

Most people and families procrastinate when it comes to estate planning, with most people thinking that they have plenty of time to get their affairs in order. However, we all know someone who has experienced the unexpected, whether it was a fatal or incapacitating car accident, an unknown or unexpected medical condition, or some other unanticipated event. **It is a myth that estate planning is only necessary for older individuals or people with a lot of money or other assets.**

Estate Planning Involves Protecting What You Own

You have probably worked hard to accumulate what you have. If you do not plan properly, your assets could be taken away. For example, if you go into a nursing home, you could spend thousands of dollars each month on your care. If you do not plan for your possible future incapacity, your estate could be squandered away in a court-supervised guardianship proceeding. Furthermore, if you do not manage your retirement account(s) properly, you could pay unnecessary income taxes. With all the lawsuits in America today, it is even possible that you could be successfully sued, resulting in someone taking your entire estate from you.

You can protect what you own while you are alive by:

- Protecting your assets from nursing home expenses;
- Minimizing your income tax;
- Avoiding a court-supervised guardianship in the event of your incapacity; and
- Protecting your assets if you are sued.

Estate Planning Includes Taking Action to Protect Your Surviving Spouse

You might be thinking that you want to make sure your spouse has financial security when you die. The Texas laws that apply when a married person dies often benefit the children more than the surviving spouse. It is important for you to plan proactively so that you can give your surviving spouse the security they need.

Example: Bob inherited stock in ABC, Inc. from his parents. Bob and his wife, Mary, are using the dividends from the stock to pay their monthly expenses. While Bob knows that he would want Mary to continue receiving dividends from the stock if he dies first, Bob never takes any action to put an estate plan in place to protect Mary. Because Bob had taken no action to protect Mary, all the stock Bob inherited went to Bob's children when he died unexpectedly, and Mary was left with nothing.

There was also the issue of their home. Even though both Bob and Mary had their names on the title to the home, because they had not put a plan in place that stated their specific wishes, the home was not automatically Mary's when Bob passed away. When Mary went to sell the home, she discovered that, when two or more people are listed as owners on a deed in Texas, even if those people are married, the home does not automatically pass to the surviving spouse. Since Bob and Mary did not establish an estate plan, Mary had to hire an attorney and go through a court process to determine whether Mary had authority to sell the home. Prior planning can prevent the courts from making decisions on your behalf and will allow you to ensure your spouse has protection according to your wishes when you pass away.

READER ALERT: Even though Texas is a community property state, your home does not automatically pass to your surviving spouse when you die - even if you have a will in place.

Estate Planning can protect your spouse by:

- Arranging for your assets to be immediately available to your spouse after you die, as opposed to going to your children or to others and instead of involving the court to determine and authorize the outcome of where your assets will go;

- Arranging your affairs so your spouse will have the freedom to sell your real estate or other assets after you die (without requiring permission from the court, hiring attorneys, or being subject to court proceedings); and

- Eliminating the possibility that your children could force your spouse to sell assets or pay them their inheritance immediately.

ESTATE PLANNING INVOLVES TAKING ACTION TO PROTECT YOUR CHILDREN

You have worked hard raising your children and providing financial security for yourself and, if you are married, for your spouse. You may like to be able to provide one final gift to your children by leaving them an inheritance. How nice would that be to allow your children to have peace of mind in their remaining years because you could leave them an inheritance? Or maybe you ride around in a car with one of those bumper stickers that reads "I'm spending my children's inheritance." While that may be true, I bet that you would rather have your children or other loved ones inherit your money and other assets, as opposed to your assets going to the government, lawyers, or the courts.

Leaving assets to your children can be complex. Whether your children are young or old, rich or poor, married or single, you need to be aware of some important legal concepts that could jeopardize your children's inheritance. Proper estate planning can avoid these problems.

If you have young children, it is even more imperative that you have an estate plan. If you die before your children reach the age of eighteen, and you do not have the proper people and planning documents in place, a judge will determine who will raise your children until they reach eighteen years of age. A judge will also determine who will control any financial assets that your children are going to receive from you when you die. All of these court decisions are made without your input as to who will receive your assets and, if applicable, how your minor children will be raised - including where and with whom they will live. Moreover, without an estate plan in place, once your children reach the age of eighteen (and in certain cases, the age of twenty-one), they will receive a full distribution of any assets they inherited as a result of your passing. Very few parents want their children to have access to all of their inheritance at such a young age.

Take action to protect your children:

- If your children are minors or have special needs, set up an estate plan so the court-supervised guardianship proceeding is avoided and *you* dictate who will raise your children and oversee their inheritance.

- If your children are older, take action to avoid leaving assets to your daughter-in-law or your son-in-law, particularly if your children get divorced or may become divorced in the future.

- Arrange your affairs to avoid unnecessary taxes.

- Protect the inheritance for your children - especially if you are in a second marriage and you or your spouse have children from a prior marriage.

READER ALERT: Without a proper estate plan, your children could have access to all the assets they inherit from you as soon as they turn eighteen.

WHAT HAPPENS IF THERE IS NO ESTATE PLAN?

If you are disabled and are unable to make financial decisions on your own because of a mental or physical incapacity, the court system - *not* your family - will decide who will control your assets and make decisions on your behalf. If you die without an estate plan, your assets will be distributed according to Texas probate and intestate laws. Unfortunately, the court system does not consider your individual circumstances or desires, and implementing the laws impacting inheritance could be both timely and expensive. The applicable laws may also fail to consider estate and income tax consequences. With a surviving spouse, children, and other loved ones, it is beneficial to specify, while you are alive, to whom and how you want your assets and property to be disbursed.

WHAT DOES AN ESTATE PLAN INCLUDE?

A complete and customized estate plan will not only establish who receives your assets when you die, it will also incorporate other very important issues, including the following:

- An estate plan can help you leave an intentional legacy to your family. If you want to make sure your spouse is taken care of when you die and that there are no complications, unnecessary legal issues, or unexpected expenses or delays, a proper plan can ensure that your legacy is intentional and effective.

- An estate plan will include appropriate arrangements to help your family avoid the probate process. Probate is the legal procedure by which the Court is asked to approve your will and distribution of your assets. It could be a costly and lengthy process to transfer assets out of the decedent's name and into the names of the appropriate heirs. Many factors can delay the process, and it can take months – or even years – to conclude.

- An estate plan may include a revocable living trust. A revocable living trust is a legal document similar to a will, except probate and other court proceedings are not required to turn property over to beneficiaries. For everyone, titling assets into a revocable living trust is an acceptable and valuable tool. If your assets are titled in the name of your trust, your trustee will have immediate access to your assets and will be able to quickly sell or distribute them to the beneficiaries you have named (see Chapter 5).

- An estate plan might include appropriate arrangements to avoid nursing home poverty. Nursing homes are expensive, and, without careful planning, individuals can lose their life savings with a stay that lasts only a few brief months. Most nursing home residents have their stay paid for by Medicaid. To qualify for Medicaid, you must meet specific income and asset limits. Without proper legal advice, you may be told that you must spend down your assets until you have reduced your savings to the point of poverty to qualify for Medicaid coverage of your nursing home bills. At THOMAS-WALTERS, our clients are educated and advised on ways to protect their assets in order to qualify for Medicaid and not be penalized (see Chapter 6).

- An estate plan will include decisions regarding the type of life-prolonging medical care you want to receive. With a living will, you can tell your family and your doctors what your wishes are regarding life support machines so your family does not have to make that final decision. When you do not write down your desires about medical treatment, these important matters could be placed in the hands of doctors, estranged family members, or even judges, all of whom know very little (or even nothing) about your preferences (see Chapter 9).

- An estate plan will include designations of the individuals who can make decisions for your medical needs or manage your financial matters. If you fail to incorporate incapacity planning into your estate planning program, your family will be burdened with a court proceeding whereby a judge must declare you incompetent and select a legal guardian for you while you are alive, but unable to make decisions for yourself (see Chapter 8).

- An estate plan will include provisions for family members who are financially irresponsible. You have worked hard to build your estate and you do not want to give it to family members who will not make mature financial decisions. By leaving their inheritance in a trust, you can control when and how they receive their inheritance (see Chapters 4 and 5).

- An estate plan will include provisions for individuals with special needs without jeopardizing government benefits. A special needs trust is an effective tool to provide for the current and future benefit of a disabled individual. The assets in this type of trust will not impact the individual from qualifying for government benefits, and these assets can serve as a secondary source to supplement the individual's government assistance (see Chapter 4).
- An estate plan will include specific asset distribution for your loved ones when a blended family is involved. Dispersing assets in blended families can be complicated. Without a customized plan in place, you have no way of making sure that what you want to happen to your assets after your death will actually happen. Prior planning can eliminate tension, hard feelings, and discord among your family members at the time of your death (see Chapter 4).

- An estate plan will include proper tax planning. Several federal tax law exemptions and deductions allow you to leave individuals and charities large portions of your property free of estate and other taxes. With guidance from an estate planning attorney who is knowledgeable in federal and state tax laws, you can preserve more of your hard-earned assets for your heirs.

- An estate plan will include an ongoing, lifetime of service without future legal charges as part of the complementary THOMAS-WALTERS Lifetime Lawyer Program. Unexpected events can affect your family dynamics and impact your estate plan. Also, law changes are inevitable and uncontrollable. At your request, the attorneys at THOMAS-WALTERS will make the revisions necessary to implement these changes in your estate plan.

- An estate plan includes provisions that will ensure that your assets will be distributed to your loved ones as quickly and painlessly as possible.

When Is the Best Time to Plan an Estate?

Life rarely happens as we expected or planned. Everyone knows that real life is not perfect and rarely goes according to the best-laid plans. Therefore, there is no better time than the present to take care of these essential issues. No one likes to think of their own mortality, but many families are caught off guard and unprepared when incapacity or death occurs. Knowing that your instructions and desires are thoughtfully planned and in place will not only protect your family but will give you and your loved ones peace of mind. Developing a unique and comprehensive estate plan is one of the most mindful and considerate things you can do for yourself and your family.

Preparing today with an effective estate plan does not mean that you will die tomorrow, just as buying car insurance today does not mean you will have an automobile accident next week. What it does mean is that, if you act now, you will not have to worry about what could happen tomorrow, or next week, or even next year to your family if your life does not follow the "normal" progression that you may have expected. Planning your estate allows you to have peace of mind. So when is the best time to plan your estate? *Right now!*

WHO CAN BEST DESIGN AN ESTATE PLAN?

Whether your estate is complex or relatively simple, having an attorney guide you is essential. At THOMAS-WALTERS, we strive to maintain the highest standards of integrity and professionalism in our relationships with our clients. We help our clients develop a comprehensive estate plan tailored to their unique needs, concerns, and goals. We believe that a well-thought-out and professionally developed estate plan will make the transitions through generations both easier and cost-effective.

Estate planning is all that we do. Our attorneys are highly knowledgeable in the field and can answer questions regarding complex estate planning issues.

THOMAS-WALTERS is with you for a lifetime. Your estate planning documents should be reviewed and updated throughout your personal or business life. There is immense value added in knowing that your customized and comprehensive plan will cover you through any and all life-changing events and law revisions.

If your estate includes property in several states, if you anticipate a move to another state, or if your children are living in different states, our attorneys can accommodate you. Our multi-state presence can handle simple and complex estate property matters. We collaborate and work together to solve all estate planning issues.

For almost forty years, we have had the opportunity to witness estate planning documents in action when a client becomes disabled or dies. Our attorneys have worked with thousands of estates, both simple and complex, and have drafted countless estate documents to deal with the everyday situations that our clients encounter.

READER ALERT. Always collaborate with an attorney who focuses solely on estate planning. The practice of law is similar to medicine – would you rely on your family doctor if you were having a heart issue? No, you would go to a heart specialist. Similarly, your estate plan should be prepared by an attorney who focuses solely on estate planning to ensure you get the most thorough and up-to-date estate planning recommendations possible.

CONCLUSION

Estate planning is one of the most important processes you can implement in your lifetime. This book seeks to explain estate planning in easy-to-understand terms so that you can make the informed choices and move confidently toward an estate plan that fits your circumstances and desires. No matter whether you have a simple estate or a complex one, with THOMAS-WALTERS on your side, you can make informed decisions and develop a smart and effective estate plan. Estate planning is an invaluable gift to yourself and your family, and it will give you great peace of mind to get it accomplished.

Chapter 2

Texas Community Property

Marriage Is an Equal Partnership – Sort Of

Texas is a community property state. Generally, each spouse owns one-half of all the community property. Our laws dictate what each spouse's rights and responsibilities are as they relate to their community property. It is important to understand Texas community property rules when considering estate planning. When a married person dies or gets divorced, these rules dictate who owns what and govern each party's rights.

Example. Ted and Ruth are married. They are both in their second marriage. Ted and Ruth, while married to each other, purchased a home, vehicles, and other community property. The vehicles are only titled in Ted's name. Ted left a Last Will and Testament leaving his home and all of his vehicles to his son from his prior marriage. Since the home and vehicle were community property, Ruth keeps her one-half ownership interest in them, and Ted's son inherits only Ted's one-half ownership interest.

Community Property and Separate Property

The general concept behind community property is that all things acquired during a marriage by either spouse are owned one-half by each spouse, regardless of who earned them or how they are titled.

Example. During their thirty-year marriage, Steve earned wages while his wife, Jane, stayed home. Jane never worked outside the home. Over time, Steve had invested in an account with $2,000,000 in assets. Even though Steve earned the money, and the account was titled in his name only, the account is community property and Jane has a one-half ownership interest in the account.

Community Property Includes:

- Property acquired during the marriage through the effort, skill, or industry of either spouse;
- Property acquired with community assets;
- Property donated to the spouses jointly;
- Damages awarded for loss or injury to something belonging to the community; and
- All other property that is not classified by law as separate property.

Separate Property Includes:

- Property acquired by a spouse prior to the marriage;
- Property acquired by a spouse with separate assets or with separate and community assets when the value of the community items is inconsequential in comparison to the value of the separate items used;
- Property acquired by a spouse by inheritance or donation to him or her individually; and
- Things acquired by a spouse as a result of a voluntary partition through a premarital or post-marital property agreement of the community estate during the existence of the marriage.

Presumption of Community Property:

Things a spouse has during the marriage are presumed to be community property, but either spouse may attempt to prove that they are actually separate property.

The Most Common Misconception About Community Property:

Many Texans mistakenly believe that, since their home is titled in their names as husband and wife, when the first spouse dies the home automatically belongs entirely to the surviving spouse. However, this could not be further from the truth. In Texas, when one spouse dies, the surviving spouse must go through a legal proceeding called probate to get the deceased spouse's name removed from the title to the home. Moreover, in the event the deceased spouse did not have a will and had children from a prior marriage, the surviving spouse may end up owning the home together with the deceased spouse's children.

READER ALERT: To ensure your surviving spouse has immediate and uninterrupted access to your home you must have an estate plan in place.

CONCLUSION

If you are married and you live in Texas, you are subject to the Texas community property laws, which essentially provide that everything you and your spouse acquire during your marriage is owned equally, with one-half of every item belonging to each of you. You will want to remember that:

- Anything you or your spouse earn during marriage is community property. It does not matter who earned it and it does not matter in whose name the asset is titled;

- The property you acquire by gift or inheritance, or property you owned before you married, is your separate property; and

- Upon the death of your spouse, you will not automatically own the entirety of your home. Without an estate plan, a legal proceeding is required to remove the deceased spouse's name from the title to the home.

Chapter 3

Wills and Probate

HANDLING LEGAL MATTERS WHEN A LOVED ONE DIES

Remember those movies or television shows where a family gathers together in a lawyer's office and a Last Will and Testament is read aloud while handing out the deceased's valuables to their relatives? Well, those days are long gone. While there are no longer public readings of wills in Texas, wills are now public documents found both in the Probate Court and available for viewing online where anyone who wants to can see all of your final wishes, a detailed listing of all your debts and assets, and your heirs. Whether you die with or without a will, if you have money in bank accounts, a home, or other assets titled in your name, your family will need to go through a probate process to pay your debts and, hopefully, inherit whatever is left over after all the court costs, executor compensation, legal fees, appraisals, accounting costs, and taxes are paid.

If you have a Last Will and Testament, you are literally asking that a court be involved in your affairs to "sign-off" on your wishes as written in your will. Probate is the court process of reviewing and approving your will, and the subsequent distributions of your assets. Before examining alternatives to this type of plan, we will review exactly what a probate is and how the process works.

READER ALERT: A Last Will and Testament does NOT avoid probate. In fact, it is more akin to a fancy invitation for your family to go through the probate litigation procedure.

In simple terms, probate is the legal court process necessary to recognize a person's death and administer their estate. If the person who died owns any property in their name, **even if the property owned is in their name with a spouse**, a probate is necessary to remove the deceased individual's name from the title to the property. Probate is a legal course of action that few people understand, but it is often a necessary one to finalize a loved one's affairs.

There are few things as devastating as the death of a spouse, parent, child, or sibling, but it is something everyone will face at some point in their lives. Family members experience tremendous grief, and, depending on the deceased's estate plan, they can also be faced with the difficulty of probate, including interacting with insurance companies, identifying assets and investments, and coping with disagreeable family members. The probate process can be lengthy and expensive for those who have a will, and even more so for those without one.

Probate can be avoided by engaging in an educational process with a THOMAS-WALTERS estate planning attorney and utilizing legal tools designed to eliminate these issues. You can read in Chapter 4 of this book about the advantages of establishing a trust as part of your comprehensive and customized estate plan and avoiding the many pitfalls of probate.

LEGAL TERMS ASSOCIATED WITH THE PROBATE PROCESS

There are specific terms and phrases relevant to wills, estate planning, and probate law. Those most common and applicable to the estate planning process are explained here.

Administrator: When there is no will and, consequently, no executor has been named, an administrator must be appointed by a judge to perform the duties of an executor.

Beneficiaries: The individuals who will receive assets from the decedent's estate, whether named in a will or, if there is not a will, as determined by the court.

Decedent: A decedent is the legal term for the deceased individual whose estate is in the probate process.

Estate: The estate includes all of the decedent's assets, such as cash, real estate holdings, stocks, bonds, life insurance, retirement accounts, vehicles, and other personal belongings.

Executor: When a valid will exists, an executor is the person who must inventory the decedent's assets, pay the estate's debts, pay taxes of the estate, file lawsuits for any claims owed to the estate, and distribute assets to the beneficiaries named in the decedent's will.

Legal Capacity: Legal capacity means that you are at least eighteen years old, or have been legally married, or are a member of the armed forces of the United States. You must have legal capacity to sign a will.

Testamentary Capacity: Testamentary capacity means that you are of "sound mind." A "sound mind" means that you understand the business you are engaged in, the effect of making a will, the nature and extent of your property, who your relatives are, the fact that you are directing the disposal of your assets, and how everything you are doing relates so as to form a plan for disposition of your property. You must have testamentary capacity to sign a will.

Testamentary Intent: Testamentary intent means that, at the time you signed your will, you intended to make disposition of your property to take effect at the time of your death.

Will: The will is the legal document that indicates how the decedent would like their assets distributed.

WHAT ARE THE STEPS TO PROBATE A WILL IN TEXAS?

Step 1: Filing with the Court. Regardless of whether a will is present, an application for probate must be filed in the probate court of the county where the decedent lived. Ordinarily, an application must be filed within four years of the date of death of the decedent.

Step 2: Posting Notice. The County Clerk posts a notice at the courthouse specifying that a probate application has been filed. This serves as notice to anyone who wants to either contest the will or the administration of the estate. There is typically a two-week waiting period before a hearing can be held for the probate application.

Step 3: Validating the Will. After the notice is posted for the requisite time, a hearing takes place during which a judge legally recognizes the death, verifies that either the decedent had a valid will or that there was no will, and either verifies the named executor or appoints an administrator.

Step 4: Inventory of Assets. The executor or administrator must catalogue and report all the assets held by the deceased individual's estate. The information typically gathered includes copies of the following:

- Statements from banks and other financial institutions showing account balances and investments at or near the date of death;

- The deed of the residence and other real estate showing the legal description of all property owned by the decedent;

- Stock certificates if the decedent owned stock in certificate form;
- The Last Will and Testament (if one exists) of the decedent;
- Titles to vehicles, boats, and trailers owned by the decedent;
- Promissory notes or mortgages owned by the decedent;
- Any mortgage the decedent owed;
- Funeral and burial expenses; and
- Documentation showing other assets and debts that existed at the date of death.

Step 5: Identifying Beneficiaries. If a will is in place, the executor notifies the beneficiaries of the estate. If a will was not filed, the probate court must determine heirship. Often, the family does not agree that the decedent's desires are accurately reflected by the court's determination regarding the distribution of assets.

Step 6: Notify Creditors. The executor must notify any and all creditors of the decedent's death and debts must be paid out of the estate.

Step 7: Resolution of Disputes. The probate court judge will hear any grievances or contests to the will before the estate can be finalized.

Step 8: Distributing Assets. After debts and expenses are paid and any contests to the will are resolved, the remaining assets are distributed to the beneficiaries.

WHAT ARE THE DIFFERENT WAYS TO PROBATE A WILL?

Texas has two kinds of formal probate, as well as a more simplistic method that can be used in limited circumstances.

Dependent Administration – If a will is not in place at the time of death, Texas law requires that the estate fall under strict oversight by a probate court. This is known as dependent administration and the administrator must seek court approval for every step in the process of settling an estate, such as posting bond, hiring appraisers, filing an annual inventory, petitioning the court for permission to sell property or distribute assets, and submitting a final report with the court. The cost of probate with dependent administration is driven up substantially with additional reports that must be filed and judicial approval that must be sought. Unfortunately, dependent administration uses up estate property and funds that would have gone to the beneficiaries. However, if there is significant conflict or distrust between heirs, dependent administration may be the preferred method.

Independent Administration – In Texas, the level of court participation in the probate process is contingent on whether there is a dependent or independent administration. Often Texas wills instruct the executor to pursue independent administration since it is quicker, easier, and less expensive than a dependent administration. If the executor is confirmed as an independent executor, he can take the necessary actions to administer the probate, such as pay debts, sell assets, or distribute assets without having to obtain a judge's approval each time. Even if the will does not provide for this type of administration, the executor or administrator can ask the probate court for authority to function as an independent executor if all the beneficiaries agree.

Small Estate Affidavit – If there is **no will** and the decedent's estate (including homestead and exempt property) is valued at less than $75,000, then those who inherit property can prepare a simple affidavit to collect the property. This is a quicker and less expensive way to transfer ownership of property; however, it does still require hiring an attorney and going through a court proceeding.

Do You Have to Hire an Attorney?

Many people question whether they are required to hire an attorney to navigate the probate court process in Texas. Most Texas courts will require that an executor be represented by an attorney in a probate matter, because an executor not only represents himself, but also the interests of beneficiaries and creditors. Texas law allows only licensed attorneys to represent the interests of others. Therefore, preparing and filing pleadings in a probate matter without the assistance of an attorney would constitute the unauthorized practice of law. Although there are extremely limited exceptions to this rule, the result is that most probate proceedings in Texas will require that an attorney be hired.

What Causes Delays in Probate Completion?

Many things can cause a delay in the probate process, including:

- The family or the attorney have difficulties determining all the assets and liabilities of the estate;
- A personal representative (executor or administrator) needs to be confirmed or appointed to handle matters during probate;

- Someone may contest the probate or disagree with how it is being managed (this could cause completion of the probate to be delayed for years);

- Either the attorney, an heir, or the family members who are in charge procrastinate;

- A federal estate tax return must be filed. This requires that certain probate assets be appraised and often requires that assets be sold to pay the tax bill. The federal estate tax return is due nine months after the death of the decedent, and often the probate is not complete until federal estate tax matters are concluded.

WHAT COSTS ARE ASSOCIATED WITH PROBATE?

The overall cost of probate will vary depending on the type and value of the assets that are being probated. In general, the greater the value of the probate property, the more it will cost. The various fees and costs associated with probate typically include:

Court Fees - Court fees alone in Texas can range from a few hundred dollars to over $1000, depending on your county of residence.

Attorney Fees - In Texas, attorneys can charge any fee they believe to be "reasonable" to probate the estate. In contrast, attorney fees in other states may be based on a percentage of the estate that is subject to probate.

Accounting Fees - These fees will vary depending on the value of the estate and the types of assets included. If the estate is taxable, then the accounting fees may include the preparation and filing of the tax returns.

Appraisal Fees - Appraisal fees are imperative to determine the date of death values of real estate, personal property, and business interests. Personal property appraisals can range from a few hundred to a few thousand dollars. Business valuation fees will typically cost several thousand dollars.

Miscellaneous Fees - Other fees may include bond fees, postage, insuring, storing, shipping and/or moving personal property.

Generally, the cost of probate will take anywhere from three percent to eight percent of your assets away from your heirs, and this amount excludes any estate or income taxes that may be due during the probate administration.

WHAT ARE NON-PROBATE ESTATE ASSETS?

Certain assets are not distributed through probate and are transferred directly from the financial institution or bank holding them to the beneficiary who is named in the policy or account documents. These non-probate estate assets include the following:

- Insurance policies
- Individual Retirement Accounts (IRAs)
- KEOGH accounts
- Pensions
- Profit-sharing plans
- 401(k) accounts
- 403(b) accounts
- Annuities
- Trust assets
- Money in Transfer on Death (TOD) or Payable on Death (POD) bank accounts

- Property owned in joint tenancy with a right of survivorship

It is important that you monitor these assets during your lifetime and properly designate your beneficiaries. Failing to properly designate your beneficiaries on non-probate assets could result in your life savings being transferred to people other than those closest to you and those of your choosing.

Additionally, many financial advisors recommend that individuals identify their "estate" as the beneficiary of these non-probate assets. By failing to name a specific individual or a trust as the beneficiary, an asset that would typically escape the probate process must now go through a probate court proceeding to determine who inherits under the individual's "estate."

Why Would Anyone Want Just a Will?

Many people want a will because they want to ensure that certain people receive their things after they die. However, what many people do not think to ask is:

- What stress does my family experience because I only have a will in place to express my final wishes?
- Do my loved ones still have to go through probate?
- How much money does probate cost and how long does it take to complete a probate proceeding?
- Does probate take money from my loved ones when I use a will as the plan to pass my assets after I die?
- Are there other more cost-effective and efficient ways to make my last wishes known and pass my assets to my loved ones?

Recommending a Last Will and Testament as a client's estate plan option, without discussing alternatives such as a trust, is common when speaking with an attorney who does not focus their practice specifically in the area of estate planning. Attorneys who do not work in this area regularly are much less likely to discuss alternatives that they have not worked with often. It is important for you to understand the emotional and financial impact on your family resulting from you only using a will. To be sure you have a plan that best fits your needs, you should discuss and understand things like:

- How your assets are frozen until the probate process is completed;
- How the probate process can take months or even years to be complete before your assets can be distributed to your heirs;
- How time-consuming, stressful, and tedious it can be for the executor you name in your will to get through the process; and
- How much of your assets your heirs will lose due to court costs, attorney fees, executor costs and fees, accounting costs, appraisal fees, and more.

There are many attorneys who do not work primarily in the field of estate planning, and it is quite common for people who work with these attorneys to report that the attorney readily drafted a will without discussing any other options. These same attorneys often claim that probate is "easy" or "simple," when most families feel lost, confused, and frustrated with the probate process. Moreover, these attorneys who only draft wills know that there is a great likelihood that the family will contact them when their loved one passes away, and they can charge the family an hourly rate to take the family through the probate process.

How Can I Avoid Probate?

Probate court proceedings can be long, costly, and confusing. Probate can be avoided by taking some simple steps while you are alive to spare your family the hassle of probate. You can form a revocable living trust to avoid probate for virtually any asset you own, including real estate and bank accounts. For a trust to be effective, the title of the assets in the trust must be changed from your individual name into the name of the trust. Because the trust is created while you are alive, it is a two-fold plan. It directs the administration of assets during your lifetime and directs the disposition of your estate at the time of your death, allowing the trust beneficiaries to receive the assets without court proceedings.

Refer to Chapter 4 of this book to understand in greater detail the advantages of establishing a trust as part of your comprehensive estate plan. THOMAS-WALTERS attorneys practice exclusively in the area of estate planning to protect your estate for your heirs.

READER ALERT: If the title of the document is "Last Will and Testament," even if a Trust is discussed in the document, this still must go through the probate process. This is not the same as a Trust established during your lifetime, as discussed in the next chapter of this book.

CONCLUSION

Probate administration often starts in a state of confusion. Survivors can become seriously burdened when information about a decedent's assets and affairs is scattered and difficult to locate. When the probate process gets underway, delayed distributions can create conflicts with heirs demanding their inheritance. One solution is to maintain non-probate assets, such as IRAs, 401(k) plans, and life insurance policies. Other assets can be held in a trust to be excluded from the probate process. Beneficiaries can receive distributions from the trust without court interruptions and expenses.

If your family does not want to go through probate, it is critical to establish an estate plan while you are alive. The estate planning attorneys at THOMAS-WALTERS can create a comprehensive and customized plan to make things as painless as possible for your heirs.

Chapter 4

Trusts

TRUSTS CAN BE GREAT TOOLS – WHEN USED FOR THE RIGHT REASONS

Trusts may seem complicated to the lay person, but when used properly, a trust can be a valuable estate planning tool. Aside from making your wishes known, both in the event of incapacity and upon your passing, some of the common uses for trusts include: avoiding probate, protecting your children from squandering their inheritance or losing their inheritance in a divorce, providing for your grandchildren's education or other needs, protecting your spouse from your children of a prior marriage, protecting your children from a previous marriage from your current spouse, protecting the inheritance of a special needs loved one, and much more.

WHAT IS A TRUST?

A trust is a legal arrangement in which a property owner (in this case called a settlor) transfers ownership of their assets to a trustee, who then manages and controls the assets for the benefit of a third person, called a beneficiary.

Think of a trust as a safe into which you put your assets, with the intention that they will eventually go to another party, the beneficiary. The beneficiary (or beneficiaries) can be one or several people, or even an organization such as a charity. Trusts are an effective tool for clients who want control over when and how their assets are used during their lifetime and how they are distributed upon their death. As you might suspect, there are many rules and regulations to be aware of when establishing trusts.

Trusts are legal documents that spell out exactly what your desires are regarding your assets, your dependents, and your heirs. Trusts are a remarkably simple concept. The trust is created, you transfer title to the assets from your name to that of the trust, but you maintain complete control of those assets while you are alive. At your death, those assets that remain in the trust are transferred to the people you have named to inherit the assets. With a revocable living trust, you maintain complete control over the assets in the trust and the terms of the trust can be revoked or changed at any time before you die. All of the property that is transferred to a trust is still owned by you and can be sold, spent, or given away.

As discussed in Chapter 3 of this book, if someone dies with a will, the will must be proven valid and probated since the will controls the estate settlement process. Without proper planning, this can be a time-consuming and expensive endeavor that could easily take many months or even years to settle. In contrast, the assets in the trust are not subject to the probate process when the settlor of the trust dies. The instructions contained in the trust are immediately executed and estate settlement costs are eliminated. Additionally, without a trust, once a probate is filed, the terms of the will and the assets of the decedent become a matter of public record. In contrast, the terms of the trust always remain private between the trustee and the beneficiaries.

In addition to eliminating the cost, time, and loss of privacy associated with the probate process, a trust can protect your assets from the hands of a nursing home. Nursing homes are expensive, and, without careful planning, individuals can lose their life savings with a nursing home stay that lasts only a few brief months. By working with THOMAS-WALTERS, you will be educated and advised on how to protect your assets by transferring them to a trust to qualify for Medicaid and avoid nursing home poverty.

DO I HAVE ENOUGH MONEY FOR A TRUST?

Many people associate trusts with the very wealthy, but that could not be further from the truth. The reality is that a trust is a helpful estate planning tool for most individuals, not just the affluent. Clients with a wide array of asset levels use our services and establish trusts to both safeguard their assets during their lifetimes and ease the burden on their family at their death.

Example. Grace lost her husband in 2015, and she has three adult children. Her assets include a home valued at $125,000, one vehicle, stock valued at $10,000, a savings account, and a certificate of deposit worth $50,000. Grace recalled that her sister and brother-in-law had great peace of mind about their future as a result of establishing a trust. Grace and her adult children met with a THOMAS-WALTERS' estate planning attorney and quickly learned about the benefits of a trust. Not only did they realize that the right kind of trust could protect the value of Grace's assets (home, stock, car, savings account, and CD) from future nursing home expenses, but they also learned that the probate process would be eliminated upon Grace's death. Grace realized how simple and systematic it would be for her children to inherit her assets if they were in a trust. Without probate, her estate would not be subject to court costs and her assets would be preserved for her heirs.

WHO ARE THE PEOPLE INVOLVED IN A TRUST?

Every trust has one or more settlors, trustees, and beneficiaries. The person who sets up a living trust is called the **settlor**, grantor, or trustor. If a married couple creates a trust together, it is a joint trust, and both are considered the settlors of the joint trust. The settlor(s) creates the trust document that contains all of the terms and directives of the trust and is completely customized to their wishes. All the assets owned at the time of death, whether in a trust or other form, are considered an estate.

The **trustee** is the individual who has the power over the trust property. The initial trustee is usually the person or people who established the trust. If you and your spouse set up the trust together, then you are considered co-trustees. When one spouse dies, the other will usually become the sole trustee.

The person who makes the trust work after you die, or after you and your spouse die if you are co-trustees, is called the **successor trustee**. The primary responsibility of the successor trustee is to distribute trust property to the beneficiaries who were named in the trust document. This individual should be someone you feel is trustworthy and capable of doing this important job.

Beneficiaries are the people or organizations you choose to inherit your trust property. The beneficiary of the trust can be any person(s) or organization(s) you desire, and you can leave each beneficiary whatever trust property you wish. Beneficiaries can be income and/or principal beneficiaries. An income beneficiary will receive everything that is earned by the principal of the trust, such as stock dividends, interest earned on bank accounts, rent from real estate owned by the trust, and earnings received from a business the trust owns. In contrast, a principal beneficiary will receive the principal or assets of the trust at some future date.

Example. In George's living trust, he made a bequest of $50,000 to his minor grandson, George III. George named his son, George, Jr., as successor trustee of this trust. George provided, among other things, that the income from the trust assets and, if necessary, the principal from the trust could be used for the health and education of George III. George also provided that if the assets had not been used by the time George III reached the age of thirty, the trust would terminate, and the remaining trust assets would be distributed to George III. When George later died, a trust account was established and George, Jr. managed the account as trustee.

In many trust arrangements, the parents are the settlors, the initial trustees, and the first income beneficiaries. A successor trustee or co-trustees are designated (often an adult child or children) and the children are designated as the principal beneficiaries to receive the trust assets after the parents die. When the parents die, the trust assets are not frozen, and trust assets do not have to go through a probate procedure to be transferred. The trust instrument and Texas trust law permit the successor trustee to distribute the trust assets in accordance with the instructions provided in the trust instrument.

What Are the Most Common Uses of Trusts?

Using Trusts to Avoid Probate:

Many years ago, it was determined that the courts and the government must oversee the distribution of a deceased person's assets to their heirs. In Texas, this court procedure is known as "probate" (see Chapter 3). Probate is the legal process that takes place after someone dies, and its purpose is to settle the deceased person's estate. It involves proving that the deceased person's will is valid or that they died without a will, preparing an inventory of all assets and debts, appraising any and all property owned by the deceased individual, paying debts and taxes, and distributing the remaining property in accordance with the terms of either the will or the laws of the State of Texas. Typically, the fees for the probate process are paid from the estate property, and these are assets and money that would otherwise go to the heirs.

Having the government and the courts oversee the distribution of your estate may not be the most efficient way for your family to receive your assets. Courts are well known for having inherent delays and costs. Most people would prefer to leave most of their estate to their children or other heirs and avoid giving a sizable portion of their assets to the court system or government.

Example. Martin and his wife, Ellen, created a Last Will and Testament that named the recipients of their property upon their death. When Martin passed away, it cost the family $15,000 to settle his estate through the probate process. When Ellen died five years later, the family spent another $15,000 on probate fees and expenses. If Martin and Ellen had worked with a knowledgeable estate planning attorney at THOMAS-WALTERS and established a revocable living trust, the family would have saved $30,000 in probate fees and expenses.

With a trust, the surviving family members avoid the time-consuming headaches and expenses associated with probate, and property can be transferred easily and quickly. Upon your death, your property goes to the people you chose and not to attorney's fees and court costs.

READER ALERT: Always work with an attorney who provides you with a fixed fee quote, in writing, prior to commencing any legal services.

Example. David wants to leave his bank accounts and his house to his daughter, Christine, but he wants to have complete control over the assets until he dies. At the same time, he does not want the $200,000 value of his house and the $75,000 value of his bank accounts to be subject to probate. David feels that it is absurd to pay thousands of dollars in attorney's fees just to have his bank accounts and house turned over to Christine upon his death. David contacted THOMAS-WALTERS and an estate planning attorney established a trust for him, with the house and bank accounts as the assets in the trust. David named himself as the trustee and Christine as both the successor trustee and the trust beneficiary. Three years later, David died and Christine turned the assets over to herself as directed by the terms of the trust. Christine avoided the delays, headaches, and costs associated with probate proceedings.

Using Trusts to Simplify the Transfer of Assets Between Spouses:

Trusts are very commonly used by married individuals. Many married couples would like for their surviving spouse to benefit from the assets accumulated during the lifetime of the couple, but worry that their assets may go to the surviving spouse's "new" spouse.

Example: Mark and Angela have $1,000,000 in assets. Mark has two children from a prior marriage. Angela has one child from her prior marriage. Mark and Angela want each other to have access to the assets whenever the first of them passes, but fear that the assets will be left to the "new" spouse if they remarry. If the surviving spouse does not remarry, there is also the concern that the entire estate may be left to the surviving spouse's child or children – leaving out the child or children of the first spouse to die. Mark and Angela decide to set up a trust so that the assets will be available for use by the surviving spouse for their health, education, maintenance, and support, and, when both spouses have passed away, the assets are divided amongst all of the children in accordance with the terms of the trust that Mark and Angela create.

Using Trusts to Transfer Out-of-State Real Estate Without Added Probate Costs:

If you own real estate in another state at the time of your death, your heirs will have to go through a probate in Texas (if there is no trust), and they will also have to go through an "ancillary probate" in the other state. The Texas probate transfers only your Texas real estate and other non-real estate assets. The Texas probate does not transfer out-of-state real estate. A probate in the other state or states must occur to transfer that property to your heirs. This involves additional bother and expense, including the process of finding a lawyer in the other state to handle the probate. If you have a revocable living trust and you transfer the out-of-state real estate to your trust, this ancillary probate will be avoided.

Using Trusts to Avoid Nursing Home Poverty:

Most people do not want to think about the possibility of spending time in a nursing home. However, a significant percentage of the population spend a portion of their life in a long-term care facility, and, if they do not plan, they may be thrown into a state of poverty. In Texas, the average cost of a nursing home stay in 2022 was $8,460 per month, or $101,525 per year, for a private room. A nursing home stay can quickly deplete your assets to the point where Medicaid would pay for your stay.

However, many people would prefer to give their hard-earned assets to their children, and not spend them on a nursing home. The solution is to create a trust to protect your assets and allow you to become eligible for Medicaid. Instead of spending your assets on nursing home care, Medicaid will cover that expense.

This type of trust is structured so your assets will not be spent or lost when you go into a nursing home in the future. At the same time, it allows you to retain some level of control over your assets and you will continue to receive all the income produced by the trust assets throughout your lifetime.

For these trusts to work effectively, they must be set up and funded at least five years before going into a nursing home. You are not permitted to remove assets from the trust and put them back in your name, but you are allowed to make distributions from the trust to one of your trust beneficiaries and they can give those assets back to you the same day, all without affecting your Medicaid eligibility.

Upon your death, the trust allows for your assets to pass to your heirs outside of probate, saving them thousands of dollars and avoiding the hassle associated with a probate proceeding.

Using Trusts to Protect Those with Special Needs - Special Need Trusts:

Many individuals have children or other relatives who are challenged by some type of physical, mental, or developmental disability. They typically want to provide for their loved one to the best of their ability for as long as that person lives. We recommend a flexible and effective tool to provide for the current and future benefit of a disabled person. This tool is the special needs trust, and it can be customized to address the unique circumstances of each family that is faced with the task of providing a secure future for a disabled loved one. By working with an estate planning attorney, the trust can be set up in such a way that the disabled beneficiary can remain eligible for need-based government benefits in addition to receiving inherited assets when their relative dies. The family's private assets serve as a secondary source of support to supplement the government benefits the individual receives.

Using Trusts to Protect Assets for Troubled Heirs:

Often restrictions on adult children's inheritance are not only advisable, but essential. If you have a child or grandchild who is financially irresponsible or troubled by drugs or alcohol, there is a good chance that you are already worried about future decisions regarding their inheritance. Giving them substantial sums of money can make bad situations worse. You do not want to enable destructive behavior or throw away your hard-earned assets. Providing for troubled heirs can be a difficult consideration when establishing your estate plan. There are a variety of approaches that can be taken to protect your assets and loved ones in these situations.

Fortunately, trusts are an estate planning tool that allow you to provide an inheritance to a troubled heir while maintaining control over when and how the heir takes possession of their funds. There are a number of different ways this can be part of a comprehensive and effective estate plan.

An individual may restrict access by naming a successor trustee to distribute the inheritance at their discretion, and at the times and in the amounts that they believe are appropriate. In this situation, the successor trustee bears a large responsibility that may seem burdensome to many people. The trust distributions may also be made according to a fixed schedule, in hopes that if an heir squanders the first distribution, they will have additional chances to make more mature choices. Offering an incentive is another means of distributing an inheritance. Completing college, remaining clean and sober for a period of time, or retaining employment are some of the stipulations often used in these trusts.

If it is necessary to develop this kind of trust, it is advisable to seek assistance from an experienced attorney at THOMAS-WALTERS who focuses solely on estate planning. They will help you develop a customized plan that will best accomplish your wishes with respect to your troubled heir.

Using Trusts to Provide for Minor Children or Grandchildren:

If you want to provide an inheritance for your minor children or grandchildren, and you do not want it to be used irresponsibly, establishing a trust for them is a viable solution. If the children or grandchildren are minors, they must have a trustee to manage their assets for them. Upon turning eighteen years of age, it is legal to have the trustee release their share of the trust assets to them. Unfortunately, this may not be a good idea because, at eighteen, they may not be capable of managing assets and could lose the inheritance that could help them significantly later in life. Also, an early windfall may decrease their drive and motivation to pursue an education or career.

By developing the correct trust arrangement, you can direct that your assets are released to pay for education, medical expenses, living expenses, and other appropriate expenses. If this kind of trust is established, you will want to choose a trustee who will be sensitive to your child or grandchildren's needs and maturity and who will distribute the money as you would have.

Example: Grandma and Grandpa want to leave $50,000 to each of their five grandchildren (who currently range in age from two to fifteen). If the grandchildren inherit this money while they are still minors, a guardianship proceeding will be required in which a court will appoint a guardian to oversee the funds. If the money needs to be used before the grandchild turns eighteen, a judge must approve the expenditure. Furthermore, when the grandchild turns eighteen years of age, the guardian must turn over all of the remaining funds to the grandchild. A better alternative is to provide for the grandchildren to inherit this money through a trust. Perhaps each grandchild's parents could be the trustees of their trust, and Grandma and Grandpa could authorize the trustees to use the funds for the grandchild's health, education, and welfare. Perhaps Grandma and Grandpa could also provide that whatever funds remained in the trust would be turned over to the grandchild when the grandchild reached the age of twenty-five (or some other age when it is more likely that the grandchild would have matured financially).

Using Trusts to Address the Concerns of Blended Families:

A blended family includes at least one spouse with a child or children from a prior marriage. The structure of a blended family can vary greatly, and can include a husband with his own children, a wife with her own children, and even children born to the husband and wife together. In these situations, where individuals each have assets that they have brought to the marriage, they typically want to provide for their spouse's needs but also ensure their assets will ultimately go to their children.

Without a detailed estate plan, a surviving spouse can easily disinherit whomever they choose, including the deceased spouse's children. To guarantee that what you want to happen with your assets will actually happen when you pass away, it is imperative to establish a plan ahead of time. Assuming your family will "work it out" after your death is a recipe for disaster. Additionally, letting the courts determine how your assets will be distributed can be a nightmare. If you want to provide for both your spouse and your children, particularly when your spouse is not the parent of your children, you may want to structure your estate plan so that assets are left in trust for them after your death. Not doing so can lead to a tragic outcome.

Example. Linda and Richard get married at age sixty. They each have two adult children from their prior marriages. Richard wants to provide for both his new wife and his two children. He creates a will, leaving everything he owns to his wife. He also stipulates that, if Linda dies before him, he wants everything he owns to go to his two children at his death. Richard dies, and all of his assets go to Linda. When Linda dies five years later, she leaves everything she owns to her two children. Richard's two children get nothing.

Similarly, failing to establish a specific estate plan can be detrimental for a surviving spouse.

Example. Steve and Sally get married at age sixty. Steve brings assets into the marriage worth $1,000,000, including the home where Steve and Sally live. Sally's assets are less than $100,000. Steve has three children from his prior marriage. Steve wants to provide for Sally and his three children when he dies, but he does not get his affairs in order in time. When Steve dies unexpectedly, all of Steve's assets, including the home and other assets Steve brought into the marriage (his separate property) are transferred to Steve's three children under the Texas intestate laws. Sally will have no financial support for the rest of her lifetime.

A married couple with a blended family could establish a joint trust that includes protection for the children and each spouse. This type of trust can provide great peace of mind in later years and eliminate hard feelings and strife within your family.

Example. Scott and Allyson have both been married before, and each had two children from prior marriages. Scott brought significant assets into the marriage. To protect the surviving spouse and their respective children, and with the guidance of THOMAS-WALTERS, Scott and Allyson established a comprehensive estate plan that included a trust. Both Scott and

Allyson are designated income beneficiaries of the trust. Upon Scott's death, Allyson becomes the sole income beneficiary of the trust, and she can use the principal of the trust for her health, education, maintenance, and support. Upon Allyson's death, the remaining trust assets will go to Scott's children.

Engaging in this type of trust arrangement meets the objectives of both providing for a surviving spouse for the rest of their life and passing the residual assets to the children of the first spouse upon the death of the surviving spouse.

You will reap innumerable rewards overall if you have honest conversations with your spouse about your goals for the future and how you expect your assets to be distributed. If your children are adults, it may be advantageous to include them in the conversations, so everyone knows what to expect. Blended families are remarkably diverse, and estate planning for blended families can be complicated. It is beneficial to obtain guidance from an estate planning attorney who focuses in these practices to ensure that, upon your death, your assets are distributed according to your desires.

Using Trusts to Avoid Estate Taxes:

The federal estate tax exemption has increased in recent years from $600,000 to $12,060,000 in 2022. Less than one percent of families are subject to the federal estate tax. However, for those families who are subject to this tax, it can be devastating. Many individuals and couples who are facing a federal estate tax at their deaths transfer assets to an asset protection trust during their lifetime to remove those assets from their estate. Additionally, each person can transfer $16,000 each year either to an individual or to a trust for the benefit of that individual.

Example. Mom and Dad have a combined estate of $26,000,000. Even with a properly drafted will or revocable living trust, there will be an estate tax bill due to the IRS after the death of the last surviving spouse. They have three children and seven grandchildren. Since both Mom and Dad can transfer $16,000 to an unlimited number of people each year tax free, they decide to create an asset protection trust for the benefit of their children and grandchildren, and they transfer assets valued at $320,000 each year to the trust. They name their wise, responsible son as the trustee of the trust. It will be his job to manage the trust assets until Mom and Dad die, and then distribute the trust assets in accordance with the instructions set forth in the trust instrument. This strategy takes the assets out of Mom and Dad's estates and reduces the potential estate tax implications that the family might face.

CONCLUSION

Trusts are an important part of any estate plan and are vital to ensure that your assets are protected and available for your heirs. The level of assets you possess does not have any bearing on the benefits derived from a trust. However, it is important to give considerable thought to the individuals who are named in a trust, including the trustee, successor trustee, and the beneficiaries, so that you have peace of mind knowing that the distribution of your assets will be made according to your wishes.

Common objectives or benefits of trusts are to:

- Avoid the expense and time associated with the probate system;
- Protect your assets from nursing home poverty;
- Provide for a special needs child while preserving government benefits;
- Control asset distribution for troubled heirs or minor grandchildren;
- Protect children and spouses who are part of a blended family; and

- Minimize estate taxes.

The THOMAS-WALTERS estate planning attorneys and staff have years of experience establishing trusts for thousands of clients, from quite simple arrangements to highly complex plans. As part of the exclusive Lifetime Lawyer Program, customized programs are established that will cover our clients through any life changes and law revisions.

Chapter 5

Revocable Living Trusts

MAKING THINGS SIMPLE FOR YOUR LOVED ONES

While the revocable living trust has been a popular estate planning tool around the United States for decades, its popularity in Texas has increased in recent years. Generally, there are three reasons why the revocable living trust is a popular estate planning tool:

- The properly established and funded living trust avoids both attorney costs and court costs involved in settling your estate through a Texas probate proceeding.

- Distributing assets after death to beneficiaries of a living trust is faster than distributing assets to heirs in a Texas probate.

- A Texas probate may require a detailed public listing of all your assets and debts when you die. A living trust can be settled privately, without the necessity of a publicly detailed listing of your assets and debts.

What Is a Revocable Living Trust?

Example: Charlene has three children. Charlene went through a difficult and lengthy probate proceeding when her father died, and she wants to make sure that her children do not have to go through a similar process when she dies. Charlene sets up a revocable living trust, naming her three children as equal beneficiaries at her death. Charlene names herself as the initial trustee and her daughter, Karen, as the successor trustee to be in charge when Charlene dies. Charlene reserves the right to change or revoke her trust at any time. Charlene transfers her real estate and her investments into the name of her trust. When Charlene dies, Karen immediately disburses the investments and the real estate to Charlene's three children. No probate proceeding is necessary, because no assets are titled in Charlene's name that would require probate court orders to transfer the title to the assets to Charlene's children.

The revocable living trust is primarily used as a probate avoidance tool and to protect your family's privacy upon your death. Without a trust, assets that are titled in your name when you die will be frozen, and your family will have to go through a probate proceeding to obtain court orders that will instruct title companies, banks, financial institutions, and others to transfer your assets to your heirs (see Chapter 3). However, if your assets are titled in the name of your trust, your successor trustee will have immediate access to your assets and will be able to sell or distribute the assets to the beneficiaries you named in your trust. No probate or public disclosure of your assets or their value will be necessary to transfer these assets after your death (see Chapter 4).

Avoiding Texas Probate:

Many years ago, it was determined that the courts must oversee distribution of a deceased person's assets to their heirs. This court-supervised procedure is known as a probate. Having the courts oversee distribution of your estate to your heirs is not the most efficient way for your family to settle your estate. Courts are known for having inherent delays and costs. In most living trust arrangements, the parents are the Settlors, the initial Trustees and the first income beneficiaries. A successor Trustee or co-Trustees are designated (often an adult child or children), and the children are designated as the principal beneficiaries to receive assets after the parents die. When the parents die, the assets are not frozen, and trust assets do not have to go through a court-supervised probate procedure to be transferred. The trust instrument and trust laws permit the successor trustee to distribute the trust assets in accordance with the instructions provided in the trust instrument.

What Savings Result from Avoiding a Probate?

That is a difficult question to answer. There is no standard for probate costs and attorney fees in Texas. Probate costs will always include court filing costs and attorney fees. However, there is no standard for attorney fees. The only thing that Texas law requires is that the attorney fees be "reasonable," and there is no standard to determine what is considered "reasonable." As such, you can ask five attorneys how much they charge for a probate, and you will likely get five vastly different answers. Where families get taken advantage of is when there is not a clear discussion regarding attorney fees at the outset.

Example: When Emily's husband passed away, she decided that she wanted to sell their home. The home was titled in their name as husband and wife, and her husband had prepared his Last Will and Testament leaving Emily everything he owned at the time of his death. Emily assumed that she could just sell the property, but she quickly figured out that is not how it works in Texas. She was going to have to go through a court probate proceeding to get her husband's name removed from the title to the home before she could sell it. Emily had an attorney friend from her church and asked him if he would handle her husband's probate. They did not discuss how much he would charge. When the probate proceeding was finally concluded about eleven months later, she was incredibly surprised to receive a bill for almost $35,000.

When you work with a THOMAS-WALTERS' attorney, you will never be surprised by our fees. We are a flat fee law firm, and we spell out in writing the exact legal services that we will provide and the total financial arrangements necessary to get your estate plan prepared properly before we begin work on your behalf.

Chapter 6

Medicaid Planning

Avoid Nursing Home Poverty

No one wants to imagine the possibility of spending the last few years of their life in a nursing home. However, not considering it could have damaging financial consequences. The age structure of the U.S. population is expected to evolve over the coming decades, with considerable growth in the older population. The natural aging process continues to cause physical and mental deterioration; however, individuals are living longer. The truth is that most people living in the United States will spend some time in a long-term care facility, and, if they do not plan for this possibility, they could become financially devastated and thrown into a state of poverty.

Most people who move into a nursing home do so in a time of great stress. Declining health, including progressive Alzheimer's disease, a sudden stroke, or a tragic fall prohibit an individual from being cared for in their own home. The family is faced with the dilemma of not only finding the right nursing home, but also determining how to cope with the exorbitant nursing home fees. In 2022, the average cost of a nursing home stay in Texas was $8,460 per month or $191,525 per year, for a private room.

An extended nursing home stay can wipe out a family's entire life savings in a few months. Therefore, many families are interested in finding out how they can qualify for Medicaid to pay for this nursing home cost.

Example: At seventy-one and widowed, Martha was genuinely concerned about her future. Her neighbor had moved into a nursing home a couple of years earlier and was forced to spend her entire life savings of $290,000 on nursing home expenses. Martha's neighbor grew concerned that she would also lose her home. Does the same thing have to happen to Martha? Absolutely not! Martha can maintain and control her assets by establishing a trust. Martha can move CDs from one bank to another and even sell her house and move to a new one. She can be the income beneficiary of the trust so she can continue to receive interest and dividends. Martha can have comfort in knowing that her assets are protected and will not have to be spent on nursing home expenses if she must enter one.

THOMAS-WALTERS estate planning attorneys are experienced in developing customized and comprehensive programs that are set up the right way and at the right time to provide peace of mind for you and your family.

WHAT IS MEDICAID?

Medicaid is an entitlement program that is primarily funded by the federal government and administered by the individual states. A principal benefit of the Medicaid program is that it will pay for long-term care in a nursing home once you have qualified. In order to qualify, you must meet Medicaid's definition of "poor." Without proper legal advice, you may be told that you must spend down your assets until you have reduced your life savings to the point that you qualify as "poor" for Medicaid coverage. By integrating Medicaid planning into your overall estate plan, you can protect your hard-earned assets and be assured that you will qualify for Medicaid when the time comes to cover long-term care expenses. Proper estate planning guidance can provide you with advanced asset protection techniques and prevent you from making mistakes down the road.

Texas Medicaid rules contain a myriad of federal rules, regulations, and state statutes that validate the importance of working with an estate planning attorney who is familiar with Texas Medicaid rules.

Medicaid Is Not Medicare

Even though the names sound similar, the programs are vastly different. Medicare is a federal health insurance program used by individuals aged sixty-five and older. Medicare is designed to cover the expenses that health insurance typically covers, such as doctor's visits, hospital stays, surgery, and lab tests.

In contrast, Medicaid is a medical assistance program. Because Medicaid is run jointly by states and the federal government, rules and eligibility requirements vary widely depending on the state of residence.

READER ALERT: Medicare does NOT pay for long-term nursing home care.

How Does an Unmarried Person Become Eligible for Medicaid?

In Texas, to qualify for Medicaid, an applicant must pass both an income and an asset test.

Income Test. In Texas, an unmarried person cannot receive more than $2,523 of income per month, which includes both wages and unearned income, such as interest and dividends. This 2022 figure is adjusted annually to reflect cost-of-living changes. Common sources of income include monthly distributions of annuities, social security checks, and pensions. If your income is $2500, but the cost of care is $5000, in Texas you may still qualify for Medicaid from an income point of view, since your income is less than your cost of care.

Personal Needs Allowance. The amount of money that a nursing home resident on Medicaid may retain from their personal income is called the personal needs allowance. In Texas, the personal needs allowance is $60 a month for personal expenses such as barber or beauty shop appointments, toiletries, clothing, and other miscellaneous expenditures. Any income above the allowance is applied toward the cost of the nursing home care, with a few exceptions such as health insurance premiums. The nursing home then bills Medicaid for the shortfall.

Countable Assets. Many people are misinformed and hold the opinion that they will be forced to spend all of their assets when they enter a nursing home. There are strict guidelines as to assets that a person may have to qualify for Medicaid. Certain assets are countable and others are specifically excluded by law.

In Texas, a single applicant can have no more than $2,000 of "countable" assets. In any month where your assets exceed $2,000, you could be disqualified and lose Medicaid coverage, which would be an expensive mistake. It is of utmost importance to work with an experienced estate planning attorney to set things up the right way and to utilize specific legal strategies designed to protect your assets from nursing home expenses.

If you can spend an asset or convert it to cash, it is generally considered countable. Some countable assets include:

- Cash
- Bank accounts
- Certificates of deposit

- IRAs (if not in payout mode)
- 401(k) accounts
- Stocks and bonds
- Lump sum annuities
- Cash value in life insurance policies
- Real estate that is not your home
- Business interests

What Assets Do Not Count for Medicaid? Non-Countable Assets. Certain assets are considered "excluded," and they will not affect Medicaid eligibility. The primary excluded, or non-countable, assets are the home, certain household goods and personal effects, one vehicle, and funeral and burial funds and spaces.

1. **The Home**. By far the largest non-countable asset that most of us own is our home property, that you have an ownership interest in and which serves as your primary residence. This includes the house or lot which is your usual residence, all contiguous property, and any other buildings on the home property, up to a value of $636,000 (in 2022). Property is contiguous to the residence if it is touching the residential property (even corner to corner) and is not separated by property owned by others. Property separated by a public right-of-way, such as a road, is still considered contiguous. It is important to note that homestead exemption status for determining home property for Medicaid eligibility purposes should not be relied upon.

   Your home property will be excluded:

   - If you are living in your home;
   - If you are away from your home because of a medical condition, but you are keeping it available to use when your condition permits; and

- If you are away from your home, but your spouse or dependent relative lives there.

However, your home property is no longer excludable if it is offered for sale based on your lack of intent to return. Furthermore, a nursing facility resident generally cannot establish a new home property while residing in a facility since they would have never lived in the new home and the new residence would not meet the definition of home property. Moreover, the value of your home property that is in another state is generally a countable asset.

2. **Real Estate for Sale.** If reasonable efforts are being made to sell real property, then the resource is exempt. Real property includes surface, mineral, undivided interests, and life estates and remainder interests.

3. **Household Goods and Personal Effects.** You can exclude the following items, regardless of value: one wedding ring and one engagement ring, prosthetic devices, wheelchairs, hospital beds, and other items required by a person's physical condition if they are not used extensively and primarily by other members of the household. Furniture, appliances, clothing, and other items of regular household use or personal significance are excluded.

4. **Vehicles.** One vehicle per household is excluded, regardless of value, if anyone in the Medicaid applicant's household uses it for transportation. Medicaid assumes that your vehicle is used for transportation unless there is evidence to the contrary. This exclusion even applies to temporarily inoperable vehicles that are expected to be repaired and used for transportation within the next twelve months.

If you own more than one vehicle, the exclusion applies to the car with the greater equity value, regardless of which car is being used. The equity value of all other vehicles, including inoperable vehicles and antique cars, is counted. Medicaid uses the NADA "Blue Book" trade-in value at www.nadaguides.com.

5. **Burial Contract, Burial Funds, and Burial Spaces.** A burial contract is countable if it is revocable or salable and conditions for its liquidation do not present a significant hardship. However, any portion of the burial contract that clearly represents the purchase of burial space may be excludable, and some or all the remaining value may be excludable as burial funds. A burial contract is not countable if it cannot be revoked and cannot be sold without significant hardship.

   Funds set aside for the burial expenses of the Medicaid applicant and their spouse may be excluded if those funds are clearly designated for the applicant or the spouse's burial expenses. A maximum exclusion of up to $1,500 each in funds set aside is allowed for the applicant and their spouse. This amount is reduced by the face value of the burial insurance that has no cash value.

   A fully paid burial space or agreement that represents the purchase of a burial space held for your burial, your spouse's burial, or the burial of immediate family is excluded regardless of value.

6. **Term Life Insurance.** Term life insurance has no cash value (i.e., the owner cannot borrow against or surrender the life insurance policy for cash). Therefore, term life insurance is not a countable resource regardless of the amount of the policy's death benefit. However, the cash value of a whole life policy is a countable resource.

7. **Business Property Essential to Self-Support.** Property essential to self-support that is used in a person's trade or business is excluded from resources regardless of value or rate of return. Excludable business properties are tangible business assets, including, but not limited to, land and buildings, equipment and supplies, inventory, livestock, motor vehicles, and all liquid assets needed for the business. Personal property used in a person's trade or business is also excluded from resources. Excluded personal property includes, but is not limited to, tools, safety equipment, and uniforms. To be considered as an excludable resource, business property (including personal, business-related property) must be in current use in the person's trade, business, or employment. If the property is not in current use, the property is excluded only if it has been previously used by the person, and if it is reasonable to expect that it will be used again. Importantly, if the business property is not directly owned by the Medicaid applicant or spouse (i.e., owned by a partnership, corporation or trust), the business property will not be excluded as a resource.

8. **Livestock.** Livestock maintained as part of a trade, business, or exclusively for home consumption is not counted as a resource; otherwise, the livestock's current market value is a countable resource.

9. **Retirement Benefits**. Retirement plans, such as 401(k) and 403(b) accounts, IRAs, and other qualified and non-qualified retirement plans, are countable resources. It does not matter whether the plan is in the name of the Medicaid applicant or the spouse. However, if the retirement plan is unavailable for withdrawal, the assets are excluded for Medicaid eligibility purposes. If funds can be made available only through a loan, termination of employment, or a hardship approved by the plan administrator, the funds are not considered available.

What Is the Income Rule If You Are Married? If you are married and receiving Medicaid benefits, some of your income can be paid to support your spouse. The income and asset tests are significantly different if one spouse is in the nursing home (the "institutionalized spouse") and the other spouse stays at home or in the community (the "community spouse"). One rule that is rarely understood is that the income of the community spouse is never considered in determining eligibility for an institutionalized spouse.

Example. Mary Smith is applying for Medicaid. Her husband receives $4,000 of monthly pension and social security income. Mary receives $600 of monthly social security income. Bill's $4,000 of monthly income is not considered in determining Mary's Medicaid eligibility.

Ownership of income for each spouse is determined without regard to Texas community property laws. A spouse has full ownership of income paid to his name; a spouse has half ownership of income paid in the names of both spouses; and a spouse has pro rata ownership of income paid in the names of either one or both spouses and another individual.

The amount of the institutionalized spouse's income that a community spouse can keep to live is called the Maintenance Needs Allowance. The following example is provided to determine how this is calculated.

Example. Bill Smith has $2,100 of monthly income and his wife Mary has $1,100 of monthly income. Bill is in the nursing home, and Mary wants to know if she can keep any of Bill's income. We start by determining Bill's income ($2,100) and deduct his personal needs allowance ($60) and his health insurance premiums ($150). Bill's liability as the institutionalized spouse then totals $1,890. Next, we subtract the community spouse's monthly income ($1,100) from the Spouse's Maintenance Needs Allowance ($3,435 a month for the year 2022) to determine how much of Bill's income Mary can keep, and anything remaining would be paid to the nursing home.

What Is the Asset Rule If You Are Married? To qualify for Medicaid if you are single, you must have no more than $2,000 of countable assets. The asset rules are quite different for married couples when one spouse is in the nursing home (institutionalized spouse) and one spouse is at home (community spouse).

In Texas, a married couple can possess as much as $137,400 (for 2022) in countable assets and the institutionalized spouse can still qualify for Medicaid. This amount is called the Spousal Protected Resource Amount. It is defined as the maximum amount of the couple's combined countable resources that may be allocated to the community spouse.

A married couple's countable assets are defined as including the community spouse's assets, the institutionalized spouse's assets, and the couple's shared assets.

Example. In addition to their home and car, Bill and Mary Smith have countable assets totaling $175,000. Bill is in the nursing home. He can keep $2,000 and Mary can keep $137,400 (in 2022). Bill will not qualify for Medicaid at this time because they have "too much" in countable assets. If Bill applied for Medicaid when he and Mary had countable assets totaling only $90,000, he would qualify for Medicaid because their countable assets would be less than $137,400. However, the assets that are allocated to the institutionalized spouse that are in excess of $2,000 must be transferred to the community spouse for Bill to remain eligible.

ESTATE RECOVERY – MEDICAID CAN TAKE YOUR HOME

To help pay for long-term care services, the federal government mandated that every state must have a Medicaid Estate Recovery Program. Accordingly, in March of 2005, Texas implemented the Medicaid Estate Recovery Program (MERP) to comply with federal law. Estate recovery includes the expenditures made on behalf of the deceased Medicaid recipient for nursing home and medical costs while in the nursing home.

Recovery can only be made after the death of the patient and their spouse. After the patient dies, Medicaid will serve a notice on the family or heirs of Medicaid's action. There are several narrow exceptions in which the state will not seek estate recovery.

Example. Bill Smith is in the nursing home and on Medicaid. His wife, Mary, lives in their home. Bill was eligible for Medicaid because their home was an exempt asset (for purposes of Medicaid eligibility) and their countable assets were less than $136,400. During Bill's stay in the nursing home, he spent $150,000 of Medicaid funds. After both Bill and Mary die, Medicaid will force the home to be sold to be reimbursed for the Medicaid funds they spent on Bill.

This does not have to be the case. The government does not get to claim your home, and it will remain in your estate if you have set up a comprehensive estate plan the right way from the beginning. THOMAS-WALTERS will develop a financial arrangement that will provide peace of mind and make the transitions through generations easy and cost-efficient.

PLANNING AHEAD – QUALIFYING FOR MEDICAID

Many people who apply for Medicaid discover that they have too many assets to qualify. There are a variety of financial options and tools that can reduce income and protect countable assets. Simply transferring countable assets into non-countable assets or property can help with obtaining eligibility, but may not protect your assets for your heirs. Seeking the advice of an experienced estate planning attorney who is knowledgeable about Medicaid is essential to properly transfer countable assets so they are inaccessible to you and Medicaid. This can be accomplished with either a timely gift or by placing the assets in a trust.

Gifting Assets. Making gifts to qualify for Medicaid is one of the most misunderstood and complicated aspects of Medicaid Planning. If you take the correct action to structure your estate properly and stay out of the nursing home for five years after you set things up, you can protect your estate.

Five-Year Rule and Penalties for Transfers. The federal government has established a period of ineligibility for Medicaid for any individual who transfers assets before applying for Medicaid. When you apply for Medicaid, you must list any transfers or gifts you have made to an individual or a trust in the prior five years. If a transfer is discovered during this five year "look back" period, the applicant is disqualified for Medicaid until the penalty period expires. The penalty period is determined by dividing the value of the transfer by the average monthly cost to private patients of nursing facility services.

Example. Mary Jones would qualify for Medicaid except that she has a bank account with $61,000. Mary decides to give her daughter, Jane, a gift of $60,000. After the gift, Mary has only $1,000. Does Mary now qualify for Medicaid? Not a chance. For 2022, the average monthly cost of a nursing home stay in Texas is $8,460. If Mary made a transfer of $60,000, she would be ineligible for Medicaid for approximately 7 months ($60,000 transfer divided by the $8,460 average nursing home cost).

What If You Do Not Have Five Years? Many people do not even think about qualifying for Medicaid until their loved one is on the doorstep of the nursing home. These people cannot wait five years to qualify, and they face the possibility of depleting their life savings before the five years expire. However, all hope is not lost; THOMAS-WALTERS can help implement strategies if this situation occurs.

To Whom Should You Give Your Assets? Your options include giving assets to your children, a trust, or a combination of the two. Most families who engage in Medicaid planning by simply giving assets to their children agree up front that the money taken out of the parents' names and given to the children will be "set aside" in an account or accounts for the children. Children informally agree that they will not touch the money until their parents die, and the children even informally agree that they will spend the money on their parents, if necessary.

Some of the negative aspects associated with transferring assets to your children include:

- Loss of Medicaid eligibility if you enter a nursing home within five years of the transfer;
- Loss of sole control over property;
- Loss of ownership interest if your child files for bankruptcy or gets divorced;
- Loss of ownership to your child's heirs if you outlive your child;

- Creation of adverse tax consequences;
- Loss of homestead exemption; and
- Loss of stepped-up tax basis.

Simply transferring assets to your heirs is not the solution. There are many disadvantages associated with this option. It is far more favorable to take advantage of certain legal strategies, including the creation, implementation, and transfer of your assets to certain types of trusts designed specifically for the purpose of protecting your assets from nursing home poverty.

TRUSTS AND MEDICAID PLANNING

What is a trust? A trust is a relationship in which one person holds title to assets, subject to an obligation to keep or use the assets for the benefit of another.

Example. John Smith has four children. John wants to give his children a gift of $100,000, but he does not want them to spend the money right away. John knows that if he gives $25,000 to each of his four children, at least three of them will spend it immediately. John feels that his daughter, Jenny, is responsible and will act in accordance with John's wishes. So, John establishes the Smith Family Trust and names Jenny as the trustee of the trust. John would like to continue to receive the interest from the $100,000, so he names himself as the income beneficiary of the trust. John would like the principal (the $100,000) to be distributed to his children after his death. Jenny goes to the bank and sets up the Smith Family Trust bank account. Only Jenny has signature authority over this account, because she is the sole trustee. John then transfers $100,000 of his money to the trust account. Thereafter, Jenny (in her capacity as trustee) manages this money for the rest of John's lifetime. She sees to it that John continues to receive the interest as the income beneficiary of the trust, and Jenny distributes the principal to John's four children (the principal beneficiaries) after John's death. Had John needed to move into a nursing home five years after setting this up, the $100,000 would not be considered a countable resource for John's Medicaid eligibility purposes.

Trusts are a popular tool in Medicaid planning because, if established correctly, trusts can permit both individuals and married couples to transfer assets out of their name, while retaining some level of control over the assets after they are transferred.

Example. In 2009, Michael set up a revocable living trust to avoid probate. When establishing the trust, Michael did not have any conversations about avoiding nursing home poverty, and necessary provisions concerning this possibility were not included in the trust. Michael suffered a stroke in 2014 and, with declining health, was forced to go to a nursing home. Michael's two children were informed that his assets were not in the right kind of trust, and over the course of the next two years, they had to spend and lose the assets in the revocable trust.

By working with our estate planning attorneys, you will gain peace of mind in knowing that your trust is set up correctly to protect you from nursing home poverty.

Owning Exempt Assets. As discussed above, your house and your car are not countable. Certain burial contracts, burial funds, and burial spaces are also not countable. By simply transferring countable assets (such as cash) into non-countable assets, you can qualify for Medicaid.

Example. Bill and Mary Smith have a home valued at $150,000. There is $35,000 left on their mortgage. They drive an old car worth $2,000, and they have made no funeral arrangements. They have CDs at the bank totaling $90,000, and their checking and savings accounts total $70,000. Mary is entering the nursing home, while Bill will stay at home. Mary presently does not qualify for Medicaid because their countable assets exceed the asset limit. Their countable assets total $160,000. But, if they use $35,000 of their cash to pay off their mortgage, purchase a better car for $20,000, and use $12,000 to prepay their funerals, their countable assets will be reduced to $93,000 and Mary will qualify for Medicaid.

READER ALERT: Medicaid Asset Protection Trusts are drafted by our office as Grantor Trusts, meaning that you are the owner of your trust and your trust will never need a separate tax identification number or have to file a separate tax return during your lifetime.

Individual Retirement Accounts. Many people have most of their money in Individual Retirement Accounts (IRA). IRAs that have beneficiaries named avoid probate, as the beneficiary's share goes directly to the beneficiary. IRAs cannot be transferred to a trust or to your children without first taking a distribution from the IRA, paying taxes on it, then transferring the money into a protected account. However, once you reach the point where you are taking Required Minimum Distributions from your IRA, only the amount that you must withdraw each year is counted if you must go into a nursing home. We have conversations with our clients regarding their IRAs as part of their comprehensive estate plan and how best to structure their plan based on their assets and goals.

SET YOUR ESTATE UP THE RIGHT WAY, THE FIRST TIME

Many consider estate planning as a complicated and confusing process. In addition, the cost of long-term care today has the potential to destroy many estate plans. It is of utmost importance that individuals work with an estate planning attorney to avoid being blindsided and overcome the fear of losing everything to nursing home expenses.

Example. Jack worked hard all of his life and managed to maintain a savings account of $50,000, and his home was worth $100,000. He was proactive in arranging his estate and met with a THOMAS-WALTERS' attorney, who educated Jack about the proper way to set things up to avoid nursing home poverty. He learned that if he went into a nursing home, he would have to spend the $50,000 in savings down to the income level to qualify for Medicaid to pay for his nursing home expenses. Jack also learned that, while in the nursing home, Medicaid would have a lien on his estate, which would include his home. Upon his death, his home would have to be sold to reimburse Medicaid for the amount that they paid the nursing home for his stay. Jack was grateful that he got his estate set up the right way, the first time. By working with THOMAS-WALTERS, he employed the necessary legal strategies to protect his assets for himself and his children, who upon his death would be able to receive 100% of his bank account and 100% of his home.

CONCLUSION

With America's population aging, the cost of care skyrocketing, and fewer government funds available, it will be more important in the future to plan for a potential long-term care nursing home stay. Every few years, the Medicaid eligibility rules change, making it harder and harder to protect your assets and qualify for Medicaid. Fortunately, there is a way to avoid losing all your hard-earned assets to the government should you or your spouse need long-term care during your later years. A knowledgeable estate planning attorney will set things up for you the right way and at the right time and make ongoing adjustments as needed in order for you to qualify for Medicaid.

Chapter 7

Designing Your Estate Plan

COMMON ISSUES FAMILIES FACE

For decades, THOMAS-WALTERS' estate planning attorneys have planned and designed customized and comprehensive arrangements for their clients. It is our priority to create a program around your family's unique needs with the same care and attention to detail as we would for our own families. We are interested in learning about you and your expectations and determining how we can best help you to achieve your goals. Al-though we have years of experience and competence in employing sophisticated techniques in appropriate circumstances, clients' goals are our focus. We strive to make the process as interactive as possible by encouraging you to ask questions. By incorporating simple and straightforward explanations in our discussions, while guiding you through the entire process, we ensure that you understand the steps and issues involved.

Most people think of estate planning as only wills and trusts, avoiding probate, and minimizing taxes. However, there are other particularly important decisions and opportunities available that can impact the lives of your loved ones after you are gone. Like you, we want your heirs to experience a smooth transition and be well taken care of in your absence.

Many of the concerns about estate planning typically revolve around the issues discussed in this chapter. We give careful consideration to these matters to get your estate legal affairs in order.

How Can I Avoid Nursing Home Poverty?

With America's population aging and the cost of care skyrocketing, it is important to plan for your potential long-term care nursing home stay. Nursing homes are expensive, and without careful planning, individuals can dissolve their life savings with a stay that is only a few brief months or years. Many individuals are interested in finding out how they can qualify for Medicaid, which pays for their nursing home costs. In order to qualify, you must meet specific income and asset limits. Without proper legal advice, you may be told that you must spend down your assets until you have reduced your savings to the point that you qualify for Medicaid coverage. Our estate planning attorneys are knowledgeable in the Texas Medicaid rules, and our clients are educated and advised on strategies to protect their assets in order to qualify for Medicaid and not be penalized.

In Texas, a single applicant can have no more than $2,000 of "countable" assets, and, in any month where your assets exceed $2,000, you could be disqualified and lose Medicaid coverage. Cash, bank accounts, certificates of deposit, IRAs, stocks and bonds, and the cash value of life insurance policies are considered countable assets since they can be converted to cash or spent. As mentioned before, certain assets are considered "excluded" and will not impact your Medicaid eligibility. These non-countable assets are a very specific set of possessions: your home, certain household goods and personal effects, one vehicle, and funeral and burial funds and spaces.

Trusts are a popular tool in Medicaid planning because, if established correctly, trusts can permit both individuals and married couples to transfer assets out of their names, yet retain some control of the assets after they are transferred. Our attorneys set up trusts that are especially useful for Medicaid planning purposes. If you transfer your assets into the right kind of asset protection trust, the assets titled in the name of the trust will not count against you when you apply for Medicaid. These trusts must be established at least five years prior to entering a nursing home. When you apply for Medicaid, you must list any transfers or gifts that you have made to an individual or a trust in the prior five years. If a transfer is discovered during this five year "look back" period, the applicant is ineligible for Medicaid until a specific penalty period expires.

It is necessary to work with a THOMAS-WALTERS' estate planning attorney to set things up the right way and utilize specific legal strategies designed to avoid nursing home poverty.

READER ALERT: Medicaid has a five-year look back period. Getting a plan in place now starts the clock ticking on that look back period, so this is one of those situations where you really must plan in advance to reap the benefits of this estate planning tool.

HOW CAN I BYPASS PROBATE?

Probate is the legal process by which the Court is asked to approve your Last Will and Testament and the distribution of your assets. It can sometimes be a costly and lengthy process to transfer assets out of the decedent's name and into the names of the appropriate heirs. Probate can take months, or even years, to conclude, and several factors can delay the process. However, probate can be avoided by taking some simple steps while you are alive to spare your family the hassle of this court process.

Certain assets, such as IRAs and life insurance, avoid probate by their nature because beneficiaries are previously designated on the accounts. Other assets such as real estate, bank accounts, and vehicles can be protected by forming a trust and transferring the title to these assets from your name to the name of the trust. A trust is a legal document like a will, except probate is not required to turn property over to the beneficiaries. You can determine when, how, and to whom you want your property distributed. Furthermore, you keep complete control and access to your property for your life, and you can liquidate and spend your assets on whatever you want or need. Lastly, upon your death, your trustee will have immediate access to your assets and will be able to sell or distribute them to the beneficiaries you named in your trust.

Many individuals associate trusts with the very wealthy, but this is a common misconception. No matter the asset level involved, trusts are an effective tool to protect your property and prevent your family's involvement in the tiresome process of probate. THOMAS-WALTERS' estate planning attorneys are knowledgeable in the area of trusts and probate avoidance and will set things up for you the right way so that your heirs can acquire all of your estate, without paying any portion of it to attorneys' fees and court costs.

WHAT ABOUT END-OF-LIFE DECISIONS?

Life is unpredictable, and to ensure that your desires regarding end-of-life medical care are carried out, it is beneficial to put them in writing. Various advance directives allow you to communicate your decisions regarding end-of-life care to family, friends, and health care professionals and eliminate confusion in the future. If not addressed beforehand, important decisions could be placed in the hands of an estranged family member, doctors, or even judges, who know little or nothing about your preferences.

Current medical advances can keep a person alive for years after it has been determined that there is no reasonable chance of recovery. Machines exist to artificially prolong the dying process. Federal and state legislatures, along with the U.S. Supreme Court, have authorized that a person has the right to die and life does not have to be prolonged by artificial means.

A living will is a document used to direct your doctor to withhold or withdraw life-sustaining procedures if your physical condition is terminal and death is imminent. As part of your comprehensive estate plan, we will create this valuable document to protect you when you can no longer communicate, prevent major arguments between family members, give you control over medical treatments, reduce unwanted medical bills for your family, and provide you with great peace of mind.

What If I Am Incapacitated?

A comprehensive estate planning program should not only include proper documentation to deal with what happens after an individual's death, but also what happens if a loved one becomes incapacitated. If you become unable to make decisions for yourself as a result of an injury, dementia, stroke, or other illness, temporary or even permanent decisions about your physical or financial situation will need to be made. If you fail to incorporate incapacity planning into your estate planning program, your family will be burdened with a court proceeding whereby a judge must declare you incompetent and select a legal guardian for you while you are alive but unable to make decisions for yourself. This public process can be expensive, embarrassing, and time-consuming, especially if your family members are in conflict over who will look after you.

Without proper planning, your family could be forced to go through the probate court system twice, once to determine guardianship and another to settle your estate.

One tool that can be effective in designating guardianship while you are incapacitated is a power of attorney. This legal document designates the person who may make decisions on another person's behalf if something restricts the person from making decisions on their own. A health care power of attorney allows you to appoint someone that you trust to be your health care agent to make medical decisions for you and ensure that doctors and health care providers give you the type of care you desire.

In the case of financial matters, a third party, such as a bank, investment broker, insurance company, mortgage lender, or other business entity, is asked to rely on the legal authority designated in a financial power of attorney. Often, the financial institution or third party will not accept certain powers of attorney if they are too old, they do not include the necessary wording, or for some other reason. If there is a problem with your power of attorney, a probate court will have to appoint someone to manage your assets and make decisions for you.

A better way to plan for incapacity is to set up a revocable living trust and transfer your assets from your name to the name of the trust. If you become incapacitated, the court cannot control your well-being or assets since you no longer own the assets in your name. They are assets owned by the trust. With a trust, you can name anyone you wish as your successor trustee to manage matters should you become incapable. A revocable living trust is universally accepted by financial institutions and provides specific instructions and directions that a power of attorney does not. This concept is simple and keeps both your family and your assets out of the court system.

By working with an estate planning attorney at THOMAS-WALTERS, your concerns regarding potential incapacity and asset protection for your loved ones at the time of your incapacity and death will be addressed and resolved.

How Can I Avoid Taxes?

Federal estate taxes are expensive (starting at forty percent), but most families bypass an estate tax obligation at the time of death because the value of your assets must exceed $12.06 million ($24.12 million for a married couple in 2022) to be liable for estate taxes. It is often necessary to liquidate assets to pay these taxes, but if you plan and create a comprehensive estate plan, you may eliminate the taxes altogether.

By establishing a trust, you can avoid paying the government certain taxes and protect your hard-earned assets for your loved ones. Also, if you give away property while you are alive, that removes the value of that property from your taxable estate. You can make gifts worth up to $16,000 per person every calendar year and avoid gift tax. However, gifted assets keep your cost basis, so the recipients will pay capital gains tax when they sell the asset, but that rate would be less than the estate tax rate if you were to keep the assets until you die. Your heirs will enjoy the step-up in basis only if they inherit assets from you when you die, not if you give assets to them during your lifetime. The "stepped-up" basis is not what you paid for the asset, but the fair market value of the asset on the date of your death. (See Chapter 10 for a more thorough discussion about taxes.)

By working with an estate planning attorney who has an excellent working knowledge of our state and federal tax structure, you can keep your family from sharing their inheritance with the government.

How Can I Provide for My Spouse?

Many married couples share a nearly universal concern that a surviving spouse will be taken care of after the death of the first spouse. Setting up their estate so that it is easy for the surviving spouse to manage things and ensuring that assets do not go to the children until both spouses die is a priority for many families. They do not want the surviving spouse to be forced to get permission from their children (or worse yet, a child's spouse) to sell or use an asset.

One of the most effective ways to control this issue is to set up a trust so that, after the first spouse dies, the surviving spouse remains in complete control of all the marital assets, without having to deal with attorneys, judges, children's spouses, or other third parties.

Postponing payment of estate taxes until both spouses in a marriage have died is a benefit of a marriage-oriented trust. The value of the assets in the trust does not matter when the first spouse dies. Even if the assets in the trust exceed the federal estate tax exemption amount, the surviving spouse will not owe any federal estate taxes at the time of the first spouse's death.

How Do I Treat My Children Fairly?

Many people initiate estate planning discussions with the intention of treating their children fairly and equally. They prefer to eliminate potential hurt feelings and perceived injustice if one sibling is financially favored over the other. However, for others, the fairest treatment is sometimes one in which children do not receive equal portions of the estate. There may be personal and other circumstances to consider prior to dividing an estate, such as the following:

- Most of your children are highly successful, except one struggles financially and you would prefer to leave them your home so they will always have a place to live.

- You may want to give a larger inheritance to a child who has made sacrifices to care for you.

- You may have a special needs child who will need lifetime care.

- Your youngest child may need support for several more years, whereas your adult children are financially independent. Perhaps your youngest child is not yet college age, and you have promised all your children a college education.

- You may have one child who has contributed to a family business and you would like to leave the business to them, while the other children who have not shown any interest in the business receive other assets.

In addition to deciding how you fairly divide your estate, you also need to consider when your heirs will receive their distribution. The timing of the distribution of your estate may vary. Your children's ages, family situations, and their level of financial responsibility are all factors to consider. Many parents prefer to keep the assets in a trust for their children instead of providing an outright inheritance. This option protects the inheritance from irresponsible spending, divorce situations, creditors, and other individuals with selfish motives who may have undue influence on your children. It is crucial that you act to guarantee that your heirs receive their inheritance in a manner best suited to their individual situation. By working with a THOMAS-WALTERS' estate planning attorney, many of these differences can be taken care of in a customized and comprehensive estate planning program.

How Do I Protect a Special Needs Child?

Many parents have children or grandchildren with special needs, either physical or mental, and they are concerned about the financial future of that child. They may be receiving need-based government benefits, and since the assistance is asset based, they are concerned that any inheritance their child receives may disqualify them from receiving aide.

Our estate planning attorneys often recommend a special needs trust as an effective option to provide for the current and future benefit of a disabled child. By placing their inheritance in a special needs trust, the disabled beneficiary will remain eligible for government assistance since the assets in the trust are not considered "available resources" for purposes of qualifying for benefits. The disabled person first utilizes the government benefits to which they are entitled. Next, the family's private assets in the special needs trust serve as a secondary source to supplement, but not replace, their government assistance. Families of all economic backgrounds rely on this public and private relationship to care for the long-term needs of a disabled person.

You may have a child who does not have special needs, but for various reasons, they may not be able to handle an inheritance maturely. Perhaps they are troubled by drugs or alcohol or have a history of handling finances inappropriately. Handing over substantial sums of money can often make bad situations much worse. You may not want to enable destructive behavior or throw away your hard-earned assets. Instead, you may want to consider leaving their inheritance in a trust and name a more mature family member as the trustee so the child will not misuse their inheritance. Another option would be to distribute the assets in the trust on a fixed schedule whereby, if an heir squanders the first distribution, they will have additional chances to make more mature choices.

If it is necessary to develop this kind of trust, it is advisable to seek assistance from an experienced estate planning attorney to best accomplish your desires with respect to your special needs or troubled child.

HOW CAN I PROVIDE FOR GRANDCHILDREN?

Typically, there is a special bond between grandparents and grandchildren, and grandparents view their grandchildren with a unique perspective. Because of this relationship, they may be concerned about their grandchild's college education, automobiles, homes, or even pocket money. Providing for grandchildren's future security may be a major priority that can easily be integrated into your overall estate plan. There are many tools available to address these concerns and allow grandparents to achieve their goals of providing for their grandchildren.

A grandparent can gift up to $16,000 a year to each grandchild and take advantage of the annual exclusion gift under the federal gift tax law. Gifts for college and medical care are exempt, regardless of the amount, if payments are made directly to the school or medical provider.

A grandparent's will or trust can include instructions to provide for each grandchild, either a fixed amount or a percentage of the total estate. If the grandchild is a minor, the assets can be held in trust with a trustee, such as the grandchild's parent, who is authorized to use the money for the grandchild's health, education, maintenance, or support.

If paying for grandchildren's education is a priority, you can place assets in a 529 plan, a Uniform Gift to Minors Act (UGMA) account, or a Uniform Transfers to Minors Act (UTMA) account. These tools are strategic ways to reduce the value of your taxable estate while working towards your grandchildren's education savings goals.

You have many options that can either aid your grandchildren or, if not handled properly, can ruin them. The methods THOMAS-WALTERS' attorneys employ as part of your overall estate planning all secure a brighter future for your grandchildren. It is recommended that you seek advice from a THOMAS-WALTERS' estate planning attorney to make sure that what you leave for your grandchildren is used for the right reason and at the right time. We want to help you maximize the benefits and minimize disappointments.

CAN I PROTECT MY CHILDREN'S INHERITANCE FROM DIVORCE?

Many clients are concerned about leaving assets to an adult child whose spouse could access them. They are concerned about the way their children are controlled and manipulated by their children's spouses.

When married children receive an inheritance, they typically place the assets in accounts they own jointly with their spouses. Inherited assets are separate property, but once the assets are transferred to an account owned jointly with the spouse, they become community property. This is not a problem if the marriage is secure, but if the marriage ends, the spouse can claim half of the inherited assets as their own. It is probably not the desire of a parent to have part of their estate inherited by a divorcing spouse.

By including a special lifetime protection provision in a trust, your child will not receive their inheritance outright, but in trust, which will keep a divorcing spouse away from the inheritance. When you pass away, your trustee can create a separate lifetime protection trust for each of your children. The trustee will distribute the inheritance to the separate trusts for each child. If the child is old enough, they can be the trustee of their own trust, which will now control their inheritance.

By setting up your estate planning program the right way, you can ensure that your children will be the ones who control and benefit from your estate, and not their spouses. You can also set it up so that, after your child dies, any remaining inheritance would immediately pass to your child's children, bypassing your child's spouse or ex-spouse. This requires careful and sophisticated legal planning which can be completed with THOMAS-WALTERS' estate planning attorneys, who have years of experience in this area.

HOW DO I ADDRESS BLENDED FAMILY ISSUES?

With the rising divorce rate in the United States, second marriages are becoming commonplace. The makeup of blended families varies, and it is important to spend time thinking about what you would like to happen with your assets after you and your spouse pass away. It is important, when you remarry, to have an honest conversation with your new spouse regarding your desires about how you want your assets to be distributed. Even though it can be difficult, the benefits of such a conversation are innumerable. Proper planning must take place to ensure that each spouse's share of the estate eventually ends up with their desired beneficiary.

You both may have children from a previous marriage, as well as children together. In addition, you may each have assets that you have brought to the marriage. Most people want to provide for their spouse's needs first and then ensure that the assets end up with their children. Consideration about specific assets that you may want to leave directly to your children may also be necessary. Disappointment and tension often exist if children do not receive an asset that they were certain their parent wanted them to have.

Atrocious outcomes can occur with blended families who do not plan properly. This is often the case when, for example, a husband (with children from a prior marriage) dies and leaves his estate to his second wife. After the husband dies, the wife creates an estate planning program to leave the assets to her children or to her next husband, thereby eliminating the first husband's children from the distribution. An even bigger problem occurs when an IRA is involved and the second wife is named as the sole beneficiary. When the husband dies, his IRA becomes her IRA, and she has the right to name completely new beneficiaries. She may exclude her husband's children from ever receiving these assets.

Many of these issues can be resolved by using trusts as part of your estate planning program. With this strategy, assets can be left to your spouse after you die, but upon your spouse's subsequent death, any remaining assets must revert to your children or other heirs. Without a plan customized to meet your specific needs and wishes, you have no way of assuring that what you want to happen to your assets after your death will actually happen. The challenges associated with estate planning for second marriages can be met by working with an estate planning attorney who has years of experience dealing with many different types of blended family situations.

How Do I Distribute Personal Effects?

Many people ask how to arrange for the distribution of personal effects upon their passing. Personal effects include such things as clothing, jewelry, furniture, china, silver, art, tools, guns, and other collectibles. Sometimes these items are part of the residual estate and are sold at the time of death with proceeds divided among the heirs. Other times, family members bicker over who gets what, causing much strife and discord. One way to eliminate future arguments is to incorporate the distribution of personal effects in your comprehensive estate plan.

Prior to meeting with an estate planning attorney, it is important to discuss the distribution of your personal effects with your family. Some of the items may have great monetary value, while others may not cost much but have great sentimental value. It is wise to determine who may want each item and, hopefully, accommodate everyone's wishes. Resist the temptation to let your loved ones make the decisions to distribute personal effects. When you pass away, your loved ones are often looking for something of sentimental value by which to remember you. If you provide for the distribution of personal effects prior to your passing, you can prevent unnecessary discord and hurt feelings among family members.

Many families have been torn apart because parents failed to address this important component of their estate planning process. Give your family the comfort of knowing that you have already addressed these concerns as part of your comprehensive estate program.

WHO SHOULD HAVE A ROLE IN MY ESTATE PLAN?

Prior consideration must be given to whom you want to authorize to act on your behalf when you die or become incapable of making decisions on your own behalf. It may be difficult to choose who to appoint to the various positions, but above all, they must be individuals who use good judgment and can be trusted with important matters.

In developing an estate plan, you will appoint individuals to serve in roles such as executor, trustee, financial power of attorney, and health care power of attorney.

An **executor** is responsible for protecting a deceased person's property until all debts and taxes have been paid and assuring that the distribution of assets is properly completed. They are charged with utilizing good faith and honesty on behalf of another.

A **trustee** is responsible for managing the assets that are held in trust. Many choose to be their own trustee if they are able to manage their own affairs. Married couples often are co-trustees, so when one person becomes incapacitated or dies, the surviving spouse solely manages the trust. When the trustee is no longer able to fulfill the role due to death or incapacity, a successor trustee is named to step in and manage the trust until the assets are finally distributed to the beneficiaries named in the trust.

If you are ill or incapacitated, the agent in a **financial power of attorney** designation will handle matters such as bill-paying and investment decisions. You should choose someone you trust completely to handle these responsibilities. The agent could be a spouse, an adult child, a sibling, or a close friend. Without a financial power of attorney, your family might have to go through a costly and lengthy court proceeding to appoint a guardian to make these decisions.

In establishing a **health care power of attorney**, you will face the important decision of naming an agent to make medical decisions for you if you are unable to speak for yourself. Most clients choose their spouse, partner, adult child, or a close relative or friend to comply with their wishes regarding medical treatment.

In naming adult children to any of these roles, it may be beneficial to consider how your other children may react if they are not designated. Perhaps it would be helpful to discuss your decisions with all of your children so your family will not be surprised or bitter in the future.

How Do I Title Assets?

The distribution of your assets is totally contingent upon proper titling. How you hold title to an asset is an extremely important decision. What is right for your friends and other family members may not be right for you. If an asset is not titled properly, there could be devastating consequences. Your estate could be subject to unnecessary taxes, assets may be required to pass through the probate process, or your family may be subject to capital gains taxes from the loss of a step-up in basis. Another unexpected consequence from improper titling of assets is that an unintended person could inherit your property.

Most people do not want to title their assets in a way that they become frozen at the time of their death. They want their survivors to have quick and easy access to their estate. Assets in a trust allow the successor trustee and the beneficiaries of the trust to have immediate access at the time of your death. The estate planning attorneys at THOMAS-WALTERS will conduct an overall review of your assets and how each is titled to make sure that your desires for an immediate and effective transfer of the assets in your estate will take place.

How Can I Keep My Financial Affairs Private?

People go to great lengths to keep their financial affairs private while they are alive. Therefore, you should consider what will happen to your records after you are gone. Without careful estate planning, your bank accounts, investment accounts, and debts will be publicized in a probate proceeding. Probate files are public court records that anyone can access. With modern technology, anyone can locate information about a deceased person's estate online. It can be quite alarming to think that, when you die, prying eyes will have access to your surviving spouse's financial records.

A trust enables you to bypass the probate process and keep your estate matters private. With a trust, you can indicate your desires regarding your assets and heirs. The successor trustee will carry out your instructions when you are gone or during a period of incapacity.

The key component to keeping your financial affairs private is to work with an estate planning attorney who will help you avoid probate and a public display of your financial records. We set things up the right way, at the right time, for every client.

How Do I Protect Myself from Lawsuits?

In today's world, lawsuits can happen to anyone and at any time as a result of, for example, an automobile accident or an injury on your property. All your hard-earned assets could be lost if a judge renders a multi-million-dollar judgment against you. You may think that automobile insurance and homeowners insurance will protect you, but the judgment amount could exceed your insurance limits or you may be sued for something that insurance does not cover.

One way to avoid losing assets to future creditor claims is to put your assets in a living trust. In Texas, certain assets such as an IRA or the cash value of life insurance are exempt from creditor claims. Regardless, it is best to plan and not wait until someone has a claim for a lawsuit against you to transfer and protect your assets. If action is taken too late, it could be undone by the court because it would be perceived as being intended to defraud a creditor. Additionally, these late transfers are considered fraudulent and may carry significant penalties.

To ensure that your money ultimately passes to your heirs – rather than creditors – it is important to work with an estate planning attorney who has had years of experience protecting assets for their clients. It is recommended to implement this protection well before you anticipate being the subject of any liability.

How Can I Protect My Pets?

Many people think of their animals as family members. They want to make sure that their pet's care and comfort continue if they become incapable of caring for them or when they pass away. One way to plan for this is to establish a pet trust, which is a legal arrangement in which payments are made to a designated caregiver on a regular basis for the care of one or more pets. In Texas, the trust will continue for the life of the last surviving pet.

Because these trusts are legal arrangements, pet owners can have peace of mind knowing that the directions regarding their animals will be implemented. The pet trust can include extremely specific information, such as a brand of food, the amount of exercise the pet is used to, and the frequency of veterinary visits. An estate planning attorney can assist in establishing a pet trust as part of your overall estate plan so that you never have to worry about the care of your beloved animal.

How Do I Incorporate Future Life and Law Changes?

Nothing ever stays the same. Unexpected events may cause your family dynamics to change. In addition, revisions to the law are constantly being made. Because of this ever-changing world we live in, you cannot expect to set up an estate plan and forget about it. You need to work with a law firm and an attorney who will support you as the law and your family circumstances change.

One thing that makes THOMAS-WALTERS unique is that our clients participate in a Lifetime Lawyer Program that provides an ongoing, lifetime of service with an estate planning attorney without future legal charges. We develop and maintain a customized and comprehensive program that will provide peace of mind for you and your family for the duration of your life, through life changes and law revisions. As a part of the Lifetime Lawyer Program, you will also take part in an ongoing educational process that will keep you current on legal matters and trends in order to keep your estate protected. Lastly, your family will have easy and immediate access to your legal documents after you die, making estate settlement an effortless experience for your heirs.

Conclusion

During the design phase, your estate planning attorney will discuss several important issues in detail and then arrange a custom solution for your estate planning needs. Some of these key issues include:

- Avoiding nursing home poverty
- Avoiding probate
- Documenting end of life decisions
- Addressing incapacity issues
- Avoiding taxes

- Providing for your spouse
- Treating children fairly
- Planning for special needs children
- Protecting your children's inheritance from divorce
- Managing blended family issues
- Distributing personal effects
- Appointing the right people to oversee your estate
- Titling your assets
- Keeping your financial matters private
- Protecting yourself from lawsuits
- Protecting your pets
- Protecting yourself from future life changes and law changes

Upon completion of your program, you will attend a signing meeting at a THOMAS-WALTERS' office to review the details of your estate plan and ensure that it is exactly what you had in mind for your family. You will be given a professional and thorough estate planning portfolio that includes all the pertinent documents and information. The portfolio is comprehensive and allows you to keep all the components of your financial arrangement organized, concise, and in one place.

Chapter 8

Powers of Attorney

WHO WILL TAKE CARE OF ME AND MY MONEY?

A power of attorney is a document that gives someone else (your agent) the authority to act for you under certain circumstances. It protects your lifestyle and those of your loved ones while you are alive, but not able to make decisions for yourself.

Example. Ronald has two children, Adam and Claire. Ronald wants Adam to handle his affairs if Ronald ever becomes incapacitated. Ronald works with a THOMAS-WALTERS' estate planning attorney and signs a power of attorney authorizing Adam to manage all of Ronald's financial affairs.

WHEN SHOULD YOU HAVE A POWER OF ATTORNEY?

You should have a power of attorney if:

- You are getting older and you want to assign a representative for yourself;
- You have been diagnosed with a serious illness;
- You have children who must be provided for if you become incapacitated;

- You have a business or property that must be maintained if you are unable to manage your own affairs.

Why Have a Power of Attorney?

There are many reasons to sign a properly drafted power of attorney as part of your estate plan:

- You will avoid the burdensome court-supervised guardianship proceeding that will be necessary if you become incapacitated. Guardianship proceedings can be expensive and embarrassing since they are matters of public record. Additionally, costs quickly mount if relatives disagree with each other.

- You can designate the person who will manage your affairs for you if you become incapacitated.

- In your power of attorney document, you can authorize your agent to engage in tax planning and Medicaid planning techniques that they would not be able to perform in a guardianship proceeding.

What Happens If There Is No Power of Attorney?

If you do not sign a power of attorney and you become incapable of managing your own affairs during your lifetime, either by accident, illness, or other incapacity, there will likely be a court-supervised guardianship proceeding whereby you and your closest relatives will be at the mercy of the court. The court will, after considerable time and expense, select a guardian who will manage your affairs and report to the court for permission to act on your behalf and for other matters. The guardianship proceeding is a burden that can be easily avoided.

Many people mistakenly believe that estate planning only involves getting their Last Will and Testament in place. However, a will does nothing for you in the event you become incapacitated during your lifetime. You need to ensure that you have the proper power of attorney documents in place, in accordance with the laws of Texas (which may differ from those of other states).

WHAT DECISIONS CAN THE AGENT MAKE?

A power of attorney allows you to specify your agent's responsibilities by designating certain powers to your agent. You may grant your agent the right to make decisions regarding the following areas:

- Real property transactions;
- Tangible personal property transactions;
- Stock and bond transactions;
- Commodity and option transactions;
- Banking and other financial institution transactions;
- Business operating transactions;
- Insurance and annuity transactions;
- Estate, trust, and other beneficiary transactions;
- Claims and litigation;
- Personal and family maintenance;
- Benefits from social security, Medicare, Medicaid, or other governmental programs or civil or military service;
- Retirement plan transactions;
- Tax matters; and
- Gifts.

In addition to the standard powers listed above, the following special powers may be given to your designated agent:

- **Power to Compel Third Parties to Recognize Validity.** This power gives your designated agent the authority to take legal action to compel third parties to recognize the validity of your power of attorney and sue for damages, both punitive and actual, in the case of a refusal by a third party to honor this power.
- **Power to Create a Trust.** This power can be used to create one or more trusts.
- **Power to Exercise Community Property Rights.** This power is used to exercise rights to manage the community estate.
- **Power over Natural Resources.** This power allows your designated agent to make, execute, and deliver oil, gas, and mineral leases.
- **Power to Appoint Substitute Agent.** This power allows the agent you have designated to appoint one or more agents as their substitute agent on your behalf.
- **Power to Pay Fee to Agent.** This power allows a reasonable fee from your estate to be paid to another individual, such as a CPA or an attorney.
- **Power Regarding Representation in Tax Matters.** This power allows your agent to represent and to appoint another agent or agents to represent you before the Internal Revenue Service or any State or other taxing authority.
- **Power over Digital Assets, Accounts, and Devices.** This power allows your agent to access, manage, modify, control, use, cancel, continue, deactivate, delete, transfer, or archive your digital accounts and digital assets (such as email, online accounts, social media accounts, etc.).
- **Power over Finances:** Your agent may have the ability to control banking, tax, government, and retirement transactions, as well as personal insurance policies and the continued donation to charities.

- **Power over Health Care:** Your agent may have the ability to consent to giving, withholding, or stopping medical treatment or services.
- **Power over Family Decisions:** Your agent may have the ability to purchase gifts, employ professionals, and buy, sell, or trade your personal property.
- **Power over Real Estate:** Your agent may have the ability to buy, sell, lease, or rent residential, commercial, and personal real estate.
- **Power over Your Business:** Your agent may have the ability to invest, trade, and manage all business decisions, as well as oversee any litigation matters.

WHO CAN BE A DESIGNATED AGENT?

In choosing an agent, you must consider your options carefully. The agent can be a spouse, adult child, or trusted friend, so long as that person always acts in good faith and on your behalf. The actions of the agent are legally considered your own actions, so you should choose a trustworthy individual. You also want to name an agent who is trusted by others in your family and who will communicate well with them.

Many clients are concerned that naming one child and not the other(s) as agent will appear as favoritism. You can name more than one agent, and it will make it easier to conduct the functions and facilitate communication. Decisions can become quite problematic if there are more than two agents. Nevertheless, many individuals with three or more children choose not to exclude any of their children from their power of attorney designations.

Typically, a married person would name their spouse as the primary agent and a child or children as alternate agents. If the spouse cannot serve as the agent, the child or children would become the primary agent(s). A letter of resignation from the primary agent, or a note from the first-named agent's physician, may be necessary for the alternate agent to act on your behalf.

For advice regarding medical, legal, financial and other matters affecting the client, the designated agent can consult experts on those matters, which may include family members with relevant expertise and/or a THOMAS-WALTERS attorney.

WHAT ARE THE DIFFERENT TYPES OF POWERS OF ATTORNEY?

All powers of attorney are not the same. You need to make important decisions before you sign your power of attorney. A **limited power of attorney** exists for the purpose and duration of a specific function.

Example. You and your two sisters inherited your parents' home a year ago, and it is now time to put it on the market. Someone has agreed to buy the home, but you are going to be out of town on the date the closing is to take place, so you will not be available to sign the documents. Two weeks before the closing, you meet with an attorney at THOMAS-WALTERS and sign a limited power of attorney authorizing one of your sisters to act for you in the sale of the property. Aside from acting on your behalf at the closing, your sister cannot take any other actions for you other than at the closing. Your sister signs her name as your agent, and you receive your share of the proceeds of the sale.

A **general power of attorney** allows a third party to perform or execute all of the day-to-day tasks and responsibilities of the person granting the authority.

Example. While discussing your estate plan with a THOMAS-WALTERS' attorney, you are asked to name the person you would want to manage your financial affairs in the future, if you become incapacitated. Your attorney explains that most people execute a properly drafted power of attorney as part of their estate plan. She describes the benefits of avoiding a guardianship proceeding. You indicate that you want your spouse to act for you if you are unable to act during your lifetime. You also state that you would like your oldest son to act as guardian, if your spouse is unable. Your attorney prepares a general power of attorney authorizing your spouse to act for you and provides that your son will act for you if your spouse has died or is otherwise unable to act for you. If, two years later, you have a stroke and it is necessary to sell your house or vehicle, your spouse (or your son, if your spouse is unable) will be authorized to sign the necessary documents to finalize the sale, if that is what is best for you.

WHAT IS A MEDICAL POWER OF ATTORNEY?

You can designate in a medical power of attorney who you would like to make your medical decisions if you are unable to make your own. You may have a living will whereby you declare your intentions regarding life support machines, but your medical power of attorney covers other important medical decisions, such as:

- Consent to give or withhold surgical procedures;
- Hiring or firing of medical personnel;
- Gaining access to medical records; and
- Visitations in the hospital when other visiting is restricted.

Example. Mike is in surgery or has some other medical condition, and he does not have the ability to effectively communicate his wishes regarding his medical treatment to his physicians. If, under the guidance of a THOMAS-WALTERS attorney, Mike previously signed a medical power of attorney, the physician can rely on the named agent to make important treatment decisions for him.

Ideally, you will name an agent who:

- Will be available when decisions must be made. The agent should be someone who lives nearby or is willing to travel to be by your side during a hospital stay;
- Will not be influenced or swayed by physicians or family members who do not agree with your wishes; and
- Understands your medical condition and any anticipated treatments.

WHEN IS YOUR POWER OF ATTORNEY EFFECTIVE?

The power of attorney that you sign will either be effective immediately or it will "spring" into effect when you no longer have capacity.

Immediate Power of Attorney. If your power of attorney is effective immediately, then the person whom you designated to act for you may do so at any time. Your agent may present the power of attorney to a bank or other third party, or your agent may be required to record your power of attorney at the county clerk of court office, and then submit a "certified copy" to the bank or third party. If the power of attorney is effective immediately, your agent can act for you at any time until the power of attorney is revoked or terminated.

Springing Power of Attorney. If you do not want to give anyone else the right to transact business for you immediately, then you may want to set up what is commonly referred to as a "springing" power of attorney, which "springs" into effect when you become incapacitated. Your incapacity will typically be triggered when doctors certify in writing that you are unable to handle your affairs. At this time, the agent who is indicated in the springing power of attorney will be authorized to act for you. A springing power of attorney typically avoids the difficult court-supervised guardianship proceeding.

IS MY POWER OF ATTORNEY EFFECTIVE AFTER I DIE?

Your power of attorney ends upon your death. No matter what type of power of attorney it is, the rights of your agent terminate at that time.

Example. Your Aunt Nelda named you in her power of attorney to manage her affairs. After Nelda had a stroke, you take care of paying her bills, selling her vehicle, and buying and selling certain pieces of real estate. When Nelda dies, the power of attorney is terminated and you have no more legal authority to oversee Nelda's affairs. If Nelda appointed an executor in her will, then the executor will have the authority to manage Nelda's affairs after her death and after the probate court confirms that person as the executor of Nelda's estate. If Nelda died without a will, the probate court will likely appoint an administrator to handle Nelda's affairs after her death. However, if Nelda had both a power of attorney and a trust in place, her successor trustee could step in immediately and oversee Nelda's affairs after she passed away, without requiring any involvement from the probate court.

READER ALERT: Your powers of attorney expire at the time of your death and the individual(s) you named in those powers of attorney will no longer have any authority to conduct business or make decisions on your behalf.

CONCLUSION

Since there is a good chance you will not be able to manage your own affairs at some point during your life, a properly executed power of attorney is one of the most important documents in your overall estate plan. Not only will a power of attorney designate who will oversee your affairs upon your incapacity, it also provides other benefits as well:

- Having a power of attorney in place may avoid the burdensome court-controlled guardianship proceeding.
- Your power of attorney can be general, or it can be limited to certain transactions.
- Your power of attorney can be effective immediately when signed or it can become effective only upon your disability.
- Your power of attorney can handle financial, health care, real estate, and other business transactions.

A THOMAS-WALTERS' estate planning attorney can effectively guide you through the process of establishing a power of attorney with your desired agent or agents. You can spend your later years with the peace of mind that future decisions will be made by someone you trust and per your wishes.

Chapter 9

Living Wills

MAKING YOUR WISHES KNOWN ABOUT LIFE SUPPORT

As you age, you may become concerned about how much pain or discomfort you will experience during a final illness. On the other hand, you may prefer to have your life prolonged rather than face the chance that discomfort will go untreated. It is an individual choice, and you are free to develop the instructions that are right for you. Additionally, you may be worried that your children will be burdened with making decisions with which they are not comfortable. Will it deplete your estate to keep you alive when that may not be your desire? This chapter discusses the importance of working with your estate planning attorney and your family to ensure that your wishes, rights, and dignity will be protected if you do not have the means of making or communicating decisions regarding your medical treatment.

Example. One day, Rebecca received a call informing her that her mother had suffered a stroke and was being rushed to the hospital. When Rebecca arrived at her bedside, she realized that her mother had lapsed into an unconscious state. Within forty-eight hours, doctors declared that she suffered irreversible brain damage that left her in a permanent vegetative state. While grappling with the horrific news, Rebecca and her brothers discussed what medical care their mother would want. They thought she had a living will, but a call to her attorney quickly revealed that she did not. To make matters worse, Rebecca and her siblings had differing opinions on her care. A living will, which would spell out what their mother wanted in medical care, would have made the decision-making process much clearer. It did not come easy, but Rebecca and her brothers eventually reached a consensus concerning their mother's care. Rebecca went home determined to have the end-of-life discussions with her family and authorized a living will so they would not have to deal with the same type of experience as she did with her mother.

As with Rebecca and her family, you have the right to control decisions relating to your own medical care, including the decision to have life-sustaining procedures withheld or withdrawn in instances where you are diagnosed as having a terminal and irreversible condition.

The United States Supreme Court, the federal government, and every state legislature have confirmed that individuals diagnosed as having a terminal and irreversible condition have the right to die with dignity and without the immense expense and misery caused by the prolongation of life by artificial means. Prolonging life through the use of machines may provide nothing medically necessary or beneficial to the person.

It is difficult to decide to authorize the withdrawal of life support machines for someone you love. Living wills allow you to tell your family and your doctors what your wishes are regarding life support machines so that your family does not have to make that final decision. You have made the decision for them in advance by signing your living will. When you do not write down your desires about the medical treatment you prefer, these important matters can be placed in the hands of doctors, estranged family members, or even judges, who know very little about you or your preferences.

Making a Living Will. You may make, at any time, a living will (also known as a Directive to Physicians and Family or

Surrogates or just an Advance Directive) that directs the withholding or withdrawal of life-sustaining procedures if you have a terminal and irreversible condition.

Life is unpredictable and often uncontrollable. Every adult should have a living will to protect themselves should bad fortune occur. There are five common reasons why you should make a living will, no matter how old you are. A living will:

- Protects you when you can no longer communicate;
- Prevents major arguments between family members;
- Gives you control over medical treatments and procedures;
- Reduces potentially unwanted medical bills for your family; and
- Provides you with great peace of mind.

Our attorneys practice exclusively in the area of estate planning and are knowledgeable in executing living wills as part of a unique and comprehensive estate planning program. Upon completion, your living will must be signed by you as a way of verifying that you understand it and that it contains your true wishes. If you do not have the ability to sign it, you can direct that someone else sign it for you.

Example. Unexpectedly one morning, Karen had to rush her ailing husband to a nearby hospital. Having done this previously with her own mother, she recalled being asked for a living will by the hospital admissions. Before leaving home, Karen retrieved the estate planning portfolio prepared by THOMAS-WALTERS and was able to immediately refer to the Living Will section when the hospital asked for the document. With all her husband's wishes included, there was never any uncertainty or question about the plan for his medical care. Despite the stress of the situation, Karen took great comfort in knowing that everything was documented and in place. Karen and her husband had spent valuable time with their attorney communicating and authorizing their wishes.

Life-Sustaining Procedure. What is a "life-sustaining procedure?" It is defined as any medical procedure or intervention which, within reasonable medical judgment, would serve only to prolong the dying process for a person diagnosed as having a terminal and irreversible condition. The term includes such procedures as intubation, antibiotic use, and feeding tubes. A "life-sustaining procedure" does not include any measure deemed necessary to provide comfort care.

If No Living Will Exists

It is common for people to enter a terminal or irreversible condition without ever having signed a living will. If you have not left directions about your health care or indicated the person you want to make the decisions, Texas law will dictate to whom the decision-making power is passed. When this occurs, the following individuals have priority to make your life-support decision, in this order:

1. The patient's spouse;
2. The patient's reasonably available adult children;
3. The patient's parents;
4. The nearest living relative; and
5. The attending physician in consultation with another physician not involved in your care.

Example. Jim, a healthy adult in his late fifties, was involved in a conversation with his attorney at THOMAS-WALTERS. He did not have a living will and expressed his hesitation about signing one. Jim's primary concern was that he might enter the hospital with a non-life-threatening disease and the living will would go into effect. What if he entered the hospital with a headache? Would all medical decisions be made based on his living will? We assured him that a living will would be implemented only if there was no chance of recovery. He was comforted in learning that a living will is acknowledged only if a patient is in a profound comatose state and machines are serving the purpose of keeping the patient alive. In addition, two physicians must declare and certify this statement of condition in writing. By working with our estate planning attorneys, Jim's concerns were clarified, and he implemented a living will that would protect him when he could no longer communicate his wishes.

CONCLUSION

As you age, you face the real possibility that your life may be prolonged against your wishes. The use of life-sustaining technology has increased over the years. With proper and wise planning, fear can be eliminated, and agony and expense can be reduced. The United States Supreme Court has stated that all individuals have the right to control their own medical treatment and that physicians must follow a person's wishes, even if those wishes are directly opposed by the patient's family. The living will, or advance directive, functions as a contract between you and your physician to either honor your wishes for medical care or transfer you to a doctor or facility that will.

Chapter 10

Avoiding Taxes

BENJAMIN FRANKLIN SAID IT BEST

Benjamin Franklin's famous words still ring true today: "In this world, nothing can be said to be certain, except death and taxes." When people think about avoiding taxes, they often think about avoiding income tax. Texas residents should be concerned about other taxes as well. Through proper utilization of estate planning tools, our attorneys can, in many cases, minimize several types of taxes, including the federal estate tax, the federal gift tax, the income tax, the capital gains tax, and the property tax.

FEDERAL ESTATE TAX

The federal estate tax applies to the estate of people who were residents in any of the fifty states at their death. When it applies, it is significant. Essentially, when a person dies, the fair market value (as determined by appraisal or otherwise) of everything the deceased owned is determined - their home, cars, bank accounts, IRAs, 401(k)s, life insurance, stock, businesses that they owned, other real estate, and much more. If the value of those assets exceeds the exemption amount ($12,060,000 for deaths occurring in 2022), there may be federal estate tax due on the amount over the exemption. The taxed portion will be taxed at a rate of about forty percent.

Future of the Estate Tax

In December 2010, sweeping new federal estate tax laws were passed. However, the new tax laws that were passed at that time were only put into effect until December 31, 2012. Congress and the President passed new tax laws in January 2013, changing the exemption amount to $11,580,000 for deaths occurring after January 2020, with the estate tax rate staying at forty percent. However, absent further Congressional action, in 2025 the exemption amount will revert to the prior $5,000,000 base, indexed for inflation.

Using Your Deceased Spouse's Unused Exclusion Amount

Prior to 2010, each spouse had an estate tax exemption. If the estate of the first spouse to die did not use their exemption, it would be lost, and the surviving spouse could not use any of the deceased spouse's exemption. This changed in 2011, and the new tax act that was passed in January 2013 allows for portability of unused estate tax exemptions between spouses. Portability allows the surviving spouse to increase their exemption amount by the unused exemption amount of the deceased spouse who died after 2010.

Example. Dad died in 2017 with an estate of $2,000,000. His estate was not large enough to fully utilize the estate tax exemption. Assuming an election was made by Dad's executor, Mom's estate tax exemption will be well over $20 million ($12,060,000 million of her own plus the amount of the exemption that Dad's estate did not use). In order for the surviving spouse to increase their exemption amount, the executor of the deceased spouse must make an election on the first spouse's timely filed estate tax return.

Calculating Federal Estate Tax

When a person dies, the executor is responsible for determining the total value of the assets that the deceased owned on the date of their death. If the gross value of the assets exceeds the exemption amount, a federal estate tax return must be filed by the executor within nine months after the death.

- If the deceased owned a business, a home, or other real estate, appraisals must be obtained and attached to the return.

- All investments and financial accounts must be reviewed to determine date of death values, and those values must be listed on the return.

The estate is entitled to deduct certain items before calculating the net estate. Common deductions include debts the deceased owed on the date of death, costs to administer the estate, bequests to a surviving spouse, and bequests to charitable organizations.

Example. Ralph died on January 15, 2019. He and his wife, Theresa, together owned a home worth $1,500,000, an investment account valued at $6,500,000, an office condominium worth $2,000,000, and miscellaneous other assets such as vehicles and bank accounts totaling $500,000. The total value of their community property was $10,500,000. Ralph's half of the community property was $5,250,000. Ralph's gross estate was $5,250,000. In Ralph's will, he left his half of the home ($750,000) and condominium ($1,000,000) to his wife and everything else to his children. Since his estate received a $1,750,000 deduction for the bequests to his surviving spouse, the value of Ralph's net estate was $3,500,000, and no federal estate tax was due.

HOW CAN I AVOID CAPITAL GAINS TAX?

A tax that is quite distressing and typically unforeseen is the capital gains tax. A capital gains tax is paid when you sell an asset that has appreciated in value. For example, if you buy stock for $20,000 and later sell the stock for $100,000, you will have $80,000 of capital gains and you must pay tax on this gain.

Step-Up in Basis. When you die, the basis of your assets will be "stepped-up" and your heirs will get a new basis. The new tax basis is not what you actually paid for the asset, but will be "stepped-up" to the fair market value of the asset on the date you died. This applies to both real estate and liquid assets.

Example. Years ago, Jane bought stock in XYZ Company for $50,000. When Jane died many years later, the stock was worth $400,000. Jane left this stock equally to her two children, so that each child received stock that was worth $200,000. Since the basis of the stock was stepped-up at death, each child will have a capital gains basis of $200,000 on their share of the stock. If they sell the stock for $200,000 shortly after Jane dies, they will incur no capital gains tax as a result of the sale.

Carry-Over Basis. This basis rule is different if you donate or gift appreciated assets during your lifetime. The person who receives the gift does not receive a step-up in basis on assets that are given to them during the donor's lifetime. If, in the previous example, Jane had donated the stock to her two children just prior to her death, the children would each have a basis of only $25,000 on their share of the stock, and they would have incurred significant capital gains tax on the subsequent sale of the stock - even if they waited until Jane died to sell the stock.

For this reason, many people choose to hold on to their appreciated assets and let their heirs inherit them at the stepped-up tax basis, rather than donating or gifting appreciated assets to heirs during their life, causing the heir to have a carry-over basis.

Married Couples and the Capital Gains Tax. The manner in which married couples structure their bequests to each other and to their family can have a significant impact on the amount of capital gains tax heirs may have to pay when appreciated assets are later sold. The fact that there is so much uncertainty about future estate tax laws does not make these decisions any easier.

It is important to be aware of the rule in community property states like Texas. When the first spouse dies, all of the community property (not just the deceased spouse's share) receives a step-up in basis to the value as of the date of death of the first spouse to die. When the surviving spouse later dies, assets owned by the surviving spouse get stepped-up again.

Example. Richard and Marie have $1,000,000 of community property. Richard died, leaving his entire estate to Marie. All of their community property receives a step-up in basis when Richard dies. Marie dies years later when these assets have appreciated in value to $2,000,000. Because Richard left everything to Marie, and Marie owned it all at her death, their children will enjoy another step-up in basis on all of the family assets.

Many people overlook potential capital gains tax when planning their estate. Structuring your bequests the wrong way can cost your family hundreds of thousands of dollars (or more) of unnecessary capital gains tax. By building a comprehensive estate plan with a THOMAS-WALTERS' attorney, you can be assured that possible capital gains tax considerations are made.

How Married Couples Avoid Estate Tax

There are many estate tax planning techniques that individuals and married couples can utilize. One such technique is to have the will or trust set up properly to make certain that each married person's estate utilizes its maximum estate tax exemption. This allows married couples who die in 2022 or later to exempt $24,120,000 from the federal estate tax, because each estate is entitled to a $12,060,000 exemption – but you do have to set things up exactly right.

Gifts of $16,000. By law, each person can donate or give $16,000 to other individuals each year without any tax consequences. Typically, no one pays income tax on a gift regardless of the value of the gift. A sizable gift, however, will have gift and estate tax consequences.

Example. Alice gives her daughter, Suzanne, $116,000 on February 1, 2017, to help Suzanne buy a home. This gift has no income effect on either Alice or her daughter, Suzanne. No tax is due as a result of the gift. The primary tax effect, however, is that Alice has made a $100,000 taxable gift. Gifts of $16,000 or less each calendar year need not be reported, but the fact that Alice gave $116,000 to Suzanne must be reported on a federal gift tax return (IRS Form 709), showing that Alice has used $100,000 of her $12,060,000 federal estate tax exemption. When Alice dies, her estate tax exemption (the amount exempt from federal estate tax) will be reduced because she used part of her estate tax exemption during her lifetime.

Many people who make gifts to others in excess of $16,000 in a calendar year do not have an estate that exceeds the applicable estate tax exemption of $12,060,000, so there is no tax consequence at all to making large gifts, other than the requirement of filing a federal gift tax return disclosing that the gift was made.

TAX AVOIDANCE TECHNIQUES

Much has been said and written about avoiding federal estate tax and other taxes at death. The increase in the estate tax exemption to $12,060,000 will exclude many estates from being subject to the tax. However, for those families that are still subject to the estate tax, the following are popular estate tax planning tools:

Prepare your will or trust properly. For many people (especially married couples), having your Last Will and Testament or revocable living trust conform to the estate tax laws will avoid estate taxes completely. Properly prepared estate planning legal documents allow married couples to exempt up to $24,120,000 from estate tax.

Make annual gifts. You can give away $16,000 to as many people as you want, every year, to reduce your estate. If you have four children and eight grandchildren, you could reduce your taxable estate by $192,000 each year by making $16,000 gifts to each of them.

Use life insurance to pay estate tax. This is a tool made popular by the life insurance industry. You are not reducing your estate tax by purchasing life insurance, but you are making gifts to children or others, and the gifted money is used to purchase life insurance on your life that might pay the estate tax liability when you pass away.

Avoid capital gains tax. Do not put appreciated assets in your kids' names without first considering the capital gains tax effect. Your heirs will enjoy the step-up basis only if they inherit assets from you when you die, not if you donate assets to them during your lifetime.

Make gifts and bequests to charity. The assets you leave to a qualified charity completely avoid estate tax. If Bill Gates leaves his entire estate to his charitable foundation (or any other charity), no estate tax will be due at his death. There are many ways to donate or bequeath money to charities - some simple and others complex.

Conclusion

You cannot avoid death, but you may be able to minimize or avoid death taxes by:

- Making sure your estate utilizes its $12,060,000 federal estate tax exemption;
- Properly setting up your will or revocable living trust, if you are married, so there will be no tax upon the death of the first spouse, regardless of the size of the estate;
- Ensuring that your heirs receive a step-up in basis - not just when the first spouse dies, but again when the surviving spouse dies;
- Utilizing annual exclusion gifts of $16,000 during your lifetime to reduce your taxable estate at your death; and
- Obtaining sound legal advice and properly prepared estate planning legal documents from THOMAS-WALTERS to assure that the assets you have worked hard to accumulate will not be unnecessarily subject to tax.

Chapter 11

Putting a Comprehensive Estate Planning Program in Place

It's Not as Painful as You Might Think

We all like to refrain from thinking or talking about death, but the reality is that death is simply a fact of life. No one is immune to the various tragedies that can strike anyone, at any time, such as illness, injury, disability, or accidents. Preparing for these unplanned events is important. It is your duty and obligation to your family and loved ones to plan for both the future and for the unexpected. Leaving them in a quandary about your estate is not a wise decision.

It is never too soon to get a comprehensive estate plan in place. By working with a Thomas-Walters' estate planning attorney, you can eliminate any unpleasant and nagging feelings you may have about this topic. The benefits of putting an estate plan in place go beyond just drafting and signing a will or trust. You can manage your assets during your lifetime and preserve your estate for your loved ones. Once your estate plan is in place, you will have peace of mind knowing that you have done what is necessary to have your affairs in order, no matter what your future or the government has in store for you.

There are eight essential steps to consider before developing a unique estate plan.

Step 1: Find an Estate Planning Attorney

Establishing an estate plan may seem like a daunting task, but the right attorney can guide you through the entire process and ensure that your property will pass to the right people with minimal delays and costs.

THOMAS-WALTERS' attorneys deal exclusively in estate planning; therefore, they are educated and knowledgeable in the details of the field. They have immeasurable experience dealing with a wide range of estates, from simple estates to complex and intricate ones. There is a unified desire to assist the client by making things easy to comprehend, as opposed to intimidating with highly technical, legal jargon.

It is advisable to identify an estate planning attorney who has published written material regarding estate planning concepts that can be used as educational tools now and in the future. Leslie Dillon Thomas, the managing partner of THOMAS-WALTERS, has authored this book on estate planning to assist clients in moving toward an estate plan that fits their circumstances and wishes.

Additionally, THOMAS-WALTERS' attorneys have authored special legal reports, blog posts, and other published material covering the many facets of estate planning. We strive to continually educate the public on the ever-changing laws and regulations relating to the field of estate planning.

Recommendations are often a reliable means of locating an estate planning attorney who is reputable. If someone you know and trust has developed a comfortable and rewarding relationship with an estate planning attorney, chances are you will as well. Unlike most estate planning attorneys, the attorneys at THOMAS-WALTERS have received countless testimonials expressing satisfaction in areas such as service quality, individualized attention, simplistic presentations, convenience, timeliness, and professionalism.

Finally, it is important to identify an attorney who has a well-trained administrative team. Our support staff participates in an extensive and ongoing training program to learn the intricacies in estate planning concepts. Both the administrative team and the attorneys work together to ensure that all client questions are answered in a timely fashion and all estate planning documents are in order.

Step 2: Meet with the Attorney

After selecting an attorney, set up an appointment to discuss what your estate plan should include. The attorney will likely make certain recommendations to you in order to complete your customized estate plan. The attorneys at THOMAS-WALTERS absorb the cost of this initial in-depth discussion about the details of your estate plan. Other estate planning attorneys charge by the hour for consultations, which can be quite arduous and costly, especially if you do not elect to hire them to complete your plan.

Step 3: Be Prepared to Discuss Your Property and Your Family

For the initial consultation, it is beneficial to provide the attorney with a general list of your assets and their values. The attorney will be able to determine if any special planning will be necessary. When you meet with the attorney, also be prepared to answer the following questions:

- If you are married, how do you want to leave assets to your spouse?
- How do you want to leave assets to your children? Do you want to leave assets to them outright or in a special inheritance trust? If you leave assets to your children in a

special inheritance trust, who will be the trustee and under what circumstances can your children use the trust assets?

- Do you want to leave a bequest to your grandchildren? Some grandparents want to leave a bequest to their grandchildren, while others want to leave it all to their children. There is no right or wrong way to do it.

- Do you want to leave a bequest to charity?

- Who will serve as your executor? If you are married, you may want your spouse to be your executor, and you may want an adult child to be your alternate executor.

- Who do you want to manage your financial affairs for you during your lifetime in the event you cannot do it yourself?

- Who do you want to make medical decisions for you if you are unable?

- Do you want to sign a living will declaration whereby you declare your intentions regarding life support machines?

Once you answer these and other questions, your attorney should have the necessary information to draft the appropriate estate planning documents.

Step 4: Work with an Attorney Who Designs a Comprehensive and Customized Program

In reality, many individuals lose portions of their estate because they did not consult with an attorney who is knowledgeable in all aspects of estate planning. The staff at THOMAS-WALTERS will explain all of the options available to you to meet your estate planning goals and to protect your assets for your loved ones.
The attorney must have the expertise to execute the right program so that not only do you have a will or trust in place, but all other relevant estate planning tools are considered.

The team at THOMAS-WALTERS is proficient in the Texas probate system. In some cases, probate is a costly and lengthy process by which the Court approves your will and distribution of your assets. By collaborating with us, the expense, hassle, and wasted time associated with a probate proceeding can be simplified and usually eliminated, leaving more of your assets for your heirs.

Developing a relationship with an estate planning attorney who is aware of the long-term care Medicaid rules is essential. Your family could potentially lose your home and life savings to nursing home expenses in the future if you are not informed of these issues. Without proper legal advice, you may believe the common misconception that you must spend down your assets until you have reduced your savings to the point that you qualify for Medicaid coverage of your nursing home bills. Our clients are educated and advised on how to protect their assets in order to qualify for Medicaid and not be penalized. Many people end up losing their estate simply because they did not talk to the right attorney.

Step 5: Employ an Attorney with Well-Defined Fees for Legal Services

Because consumers prefer it, our estate planning attorneys provide comprehensive legal services for a documented fixed amount that is communicated in advance. Most other attorneys charge for their services based on the number of minutes or hours they work on a project. Their clients are notoriously frustrated at the completion of their estate plan because they are hit with an excessive bill that includes charges not only for legal services, but also for photocopies, telephone conversations, emails, internal office discussions, and other miscellaneous fees. These clients are typically unpleasantly surprised by the total accumulated costs, but, unfortunately they have no recourse against the attorney.

With THOMAS-WALTERS, you are always encouraged to communicate openly with your estate planning attorney without the fear that you will be taken advantage of financially. Our attorneys will prepare, design, and maintain your estate planning program for your entire lifetime for a fixed amount that you are aware of from the start. We also offer guaranteed satisfaction that other attorneys simply cannot provide.

Step 6: Enlist an Attorney Who Provides Timely Service

Nothing is more disheartening than working with a professional who is not committed to your desired result. Many individuals come to us after experiencing delays and frustrations with other firms. They grow weary waiting for things to happen to complete their estate planning program. By working with an attorney at THOMAS-WALTERS, rest assured that your documents will be ready for you to sign in a few short weeks. We take great pride in customer satisfaction and ensuring that your goals are accomplished for your estate in a prompt manner.

Step 7: Utilize an Attorney Who Maintains Your Estate Program During Your Lifetime

One thing that makes THOMAS-WALTERS unique is that our clients participate in an exclusive Lifetime Lawyer Program that provides an ongoing, lifetime of service with an estate planning attorney. The customized program will cover you now and in the future, through life changes and law revisions. In addition, you will take place in ongoing educational processes with us that include newsletters, webinars, and live presentations to help you stay up to date on legal matters and trends to keep your estate protected.

Step 8: Build a Relationship with an Attorney Who Supports Surviving Family Members

The relationship established with a THOMAS-WALTERS' estate planning attorney continues with your heirs upon your death. We maintain scanned estate planning documents for all clients, and they are always available to provide immediate and easy access for your loved ones. It is beneficial to work with our attorneys and staff, who are well-trained in all aspects of estate settlement, including trust administration, various tax rules, and the probate process. Because many other attorneys are not sophisticated enough or knowledgeable in all areas of estate settlement, it is best to build a relationship with a THOMAS-WALTERS' attorney who practices exclusively in this area.

READER ALERT: Our Lifetime Lawyer Program enables you to make sure your estate planning documents always remain current.

CONCLUSION

To design, complete, and maintain a proper estate plan, there are several steps to be considered and weighed.

1. Employ a THOMAS-WALTERS' attorney who deals exclusively in estate planning, presents concepts in an understandable manner, publishes written material to keep clients educated, and is highly recommended by thousands of others.

2. Meet with one of our estate planning attorneys who will absorb the cost of the initial discussion regarding your customized and comprehensive estate plan.

3. Before meeting with one of our attorneys, develop a list of your assets and gather all deeds or legal descriptions for your real property. Also, you should consider property distribution upon your death, along with the identification of individuals who could make financial and medical decisions on your behalf.

4. Engage in a relationship with an attorney who will design a comprehensive program based on their thorough knowledge of all aspects of estate planning.

5. Consider an estate planning attorney who provides timely service for a predetermined fee.

6. Participate in an exclusive, complementary Lifetime Lawyer Program with a THOMAS-WALTERS' attorney who guarantees satisfaction for the duration of your lifetime.

Glossary

Administrator - the person appointed by the court whose duty it is to collect, preserve, and manage the property of an estate during probate. The court often appoints an administrator when a decedent had no Last Will and Testament.

Bequest - a gift to an individual or entity upon your death.

Beneficiary - an individual or entity who will receive real property, personal property, or liquid assets when you pass away.

Carry-Over Basis - the value of property as of the date it was purchased.

Community Property - property acquired by spouses during their marriage in which each spouse owns an undivided one-half interest. Texas is a community property state.

Estate Administration - the process of settling an estate after someone dies.

Executor - the person you designate in your Last Will and Testament to work with the attorney to settle your estate.

Exempt Assets - those assets that are not counted for purposes of Medicaid qualification.

Estate Planning - the process of arranging your affairs so that, upon your death or disability, your estate will be managed efficiently by the people you trust, and there will be minimal expenses or other costs.

Estate Tax - the tax your estate must pay to the federal government if your net estate exceeds the applicable estate tax exemption at your death.
Federal Estate Tax Exemption - the amount of your estate that is exempt from paying taxes upon your death.

Gift Tax - the tax you must pay to the state or federal government for making a gift for the benefit of another person.

Independent Executor - your executor who acts pursuant to a simpler probate process because you either authorized it in your will or each of your heirs agreed to allow the executor to serve as an independent executor. Independent executors typically do not require the court authorization to act that is otherwise required of executors.

Intestate Laws - the laws that dictate who inherits your assets if you die without a valid Last Will and Testament.

Last Will and Testament - a legal document naming your executor and describing, among other things, who is entitled to your assets when you die.

Living Trust - a trust that you establish during your lifetime.

Living Will - a document in which you express your intentions regarding the withdrawal or withholding of life support systems (also called a Directive to Physicians).

Medicaid - the federal and state program that will pay for all or a portion of your nursing home care if you meet the Medicaid eligibility requirements.

Medicaid Asset Protection Trust - a type of irrevocable trust that, if established in the right way and at the right time, can protect assets in the event of a nursing home admission.

Medicaid Planning - the process of taking advantage of legal strategies to protect your estate in the event you need long-term care in a nursing home.
Medicare - health insurance for individuals 65 and over, paying most of the cost for surgeries, doctor visits, and other medical expenses. Medicare is completely different from Medicaid.

Non-probate Assets - assets that are not listed in probate, such as retirement plans, individual retirement accounts, life insurance, and annuities.

Power of Attorney - a document you sign authorizing another person to act for you during your lifetime, for medical or financial purposes.

Probate - the court-supervised process of transferring your assets to your heirs or legatees after your death.

Pour-Over Will - everyone who has a Trust also has a will. This will serves to "pour-over" their personal property into their Trust when they die. It also serves as a device to ensure any real property that was inadvertently not transferred into the Trust during their lifetime is included in the Trust upon their death.

Revocable Living Trust - a type of trust you create during your lifetime, whereby you are both the trustee and beneficiary during your lifetime, and you provide who the beneficiaries will be at the time of your death. A revocable living trust is often used as a substitute to a Last Will and Testament to avoid probate.

Separate Property - property that you own that is not community property with your spouse. Common examples of separate property are property you acquired before you married, property you inherited, and property that was given to you by someone else.

Settlor - a person who creates a trust (sometimes called a "grantor").

Testamentary Trust - a trust, the terms of which are stated in your Last Will and Testament.

Testator - one who makes or has made a Will.

Trust - a relationship resulting from the transfer of title to property to a person (trustee) to be administered for the benefit of another (beneficiary).

Trustee - the person appointed to hold and manage property in trust for the benefit of another.

Will - also known as a Last Will and Testament. Your will is the important document you sign that leaves your estate to your loved ones, names your executor, and provides for many other aspects regarding the settling of your estate.

Testimonials from Clients of THOMAS-WALTERS, PLLC

"When we attended the seminar given by Leslie we were very impressed with her presentation in language all of us could understand. It was very helpful that Leslie gave real life examples to get her information across. Leslie impressed us with her professionalism, knowledge, and patience in answering people's questions. Her sincerity about the seriousness of people planning their estates and what happens if one thinks they have plenty of time and do not do anything hit each and every one of us at her seminar. We appreciated the fact that Leslie did not use 'high pressure' tactics to get our business. She gave her presentation, told everyone about her flat rate fee that is good for a lifetime of service, and then let everyone at the seminar decide what avenue they wanted to pursue."
– Andy and Sharon Mutzig

"I am very pleased with the services of Leslie Thomas and her staff. Each call or email was answered promptly and with the utmost professionalism. Leslie is knowledgeable and made a tedious responsibility a pleasant experience. I would recommend her Estate Planning services without reservation."
– Sharon Gillespie

"After hearing Leslie's estate planning presentation, it was clear that we needed help to prepare for the inevitable and make the transition as easy and cost effective as possible for our children. We had many questions, and Leslie took the time to personally answer them all. She even consulted with our financial planner to assure a comprehensive estate plan. Leslie made the entire estate planning process simple and easy to understand. Thanks to Leslie, we now have peace of mind in knowing that our children will be able to settle our estate quickly, with ease, and save thousands of dollars in the process. We highly recommend the estate planning services of Leslie Thomas!"
— Charles Horn

"Leslie Thomas is someone you would definitely want in your corner. She is personable, dependable, knowledgeable, and highly intelligent. Leslie answered every phone call and email in a prompt manner. Very impressive! We feel extremely confident and relaxed knowing we have chosen someone of her caliber to handle this endeavor. Leslie is awesome and we highly recommend her."
— Gary and Margaret Holcomb

"Leslie was wonderful to work with for all of my estate planning. She really listened to my needs and concerns. She explained everything in terms that I could understand. I wholeheartedly recommend Leslie Thomas for all of your estate planning needs."
— Linda Sawicki

"Estate planning is never easy or fun. Leslie Thomas and her staff made it as easy as possible. It took less than four weeks from seminar to delivery of our portfolio. Everything is well organized and in layman's terms."
— Pappas Family

"Ms. Thomas was very professional, thorough, and was able to manage the establishment of our trust plan in a very effective manner. I was very fortunate to have Ms. Thomas oversee my trust, and I would highly recommend her to any of my colleagues."
– Suhail Sharif, MD

"THOMAS-WALTERS has truly been a blessing to our family in preparing, planning, and maintaining our estate for the future. Everyone was personable, professional, and knowledgeable. They truly went above and beyond in addressing our needs, and explained legal terms in understandable language. We are very pleased and feel secure that our future is well planned!"
– Patsy and Donald Moore

"Totally professional...but regular people! TV and regular lawyers tend to intimidate. THOMAS-WALTERS keeps things simple, but they make sure you understand everything. After completing our last session signing everything, my wife and I left the office with smiles and feelings of relief. Also, at THOMAS-WALTERS, there is a feeling of mutual respect on both sides."
– Gerald and Doris Goodwin

"We attended a seminar given by THOMAS-WALTERS. It was presented in such an informative way that ninety-eight percent of our questions were answered! Everyone we dealt with was very professional and courteous. We would recommend this firm to anyone. Thanks for all you have done to help us in our estate planning."
– J. John Haydel

"The knowledge that our kids won't have to settle our estate when we pass away gives us peace of mind. With both of us having stepchildren, we know that by planning our estate now none of our children will be left behind, and the children will have fewer problems. Thank you for your services. We are very satisfied for the knowledge that our estate planning is done, and our wishes will be conducted."
– Bryan and Lisa Brown

"We expected the development of an estate plan to be difficult and complicated. Thanks to your firm, the guidance provided was stress-free and completed with ease. We highly recommend THOMAS-WALTERS and your practice to others."
– George and Rachel Weir

"We were hesitant to attend the seminar, thinking that the development of an estate plan was going to be difficult, time-consuming, and complicated. However, Leslie Thomas walked us through each step of the process. Everyone at the firm was professional, and the entire estate planning process was stress-free. We are comfortable knowing we have a 'Lawyer for Life' in Leslie Thomas and her firm."
– Scott and Allyson Davis

Made in the USA
Columbia, SC
27 August 2022

65500712R00074